NO BUSINESS IS TOO SMALL FOR

DIGITAL
MARKETING

NO BUSINESS IS TOO SMALL FOR

DIGITAL MARKETING

. . .

EVERYTHING YOU NEED TO KNOW TO
GROW YOUR BUSINESS

JON MARTINSEN

Published by Advantage, Charleston, South Carolina.
Member of Advantage Media Group.

ADVANTAGE is a registered trademark, and the Advantage colophon is a trademark of Advantage Media Group, Inc.

Printed in the United States of America.

10 9 8 7 6 5 4 3 2 1

ISBN: 978-1-64225-359-7
LCCN: 2022905613

Cover design by Megan Elger.
Layout design by Mary Hamilton.

This publication is designed to provide accurate and authoritative information in regard to the subject matter covered. It is sold with the understanding that the publisher is not engaged in rendering legal, accounting, or other professional services. If legal advice or other expert assistance is required, the services of a competent professional person should be sought.

Advantage Media Group is proud to be a part of the Tree Neutral® program. Tree Neutral offsets the number of trees consumed in the production and printing of this book by taking proactive steps such as planting trees in direct proportion to the number of trees used to print books. To learn more about Tree Neutral, please visit **www.treeneutral.com**.

Advantage Media Group is a publisher of business, self-improvement, and professional development books and online learning. We help entrepreneurs, business leaders, and professionals share their Stories, Passion, and Knowledge to help others Learn & Grow. Do you have a manuscript or book idea that you would like us to consider for publishing? Please visit **advantagefamily.com**.

For my partners and employees who have helped me during my work life, guiding companies to grow and get new customers.

CONTENTS

A DIGITAL WORLD OPENS UP NEW OPPORTUNITIES FOR SMBS

■ ■ ■

Y ou run a small business—a boutique clothing store, a coffee shop or bakery, a plumbing or electrical service, an accounting/investing advisory, or any one of thousands of kinds of small businesses. As a small business owner, you are busy *all the time*. On the other hand, you must sustain and grow your business in order to succeed, so you need to market it. But what kind of marketing do you need to do in order to succeed? Is a **website** enough? What needs to be on that **website**? What should it do for you? What about a social media presence? How should you be communicating with your customers, and how often?

These kinds of questions plague today's small business owners, who are already overtaxed. Because you have limited resources, you are often forced to balance the responsibilities of running your business— including marketing it—with the services you provide your customers.

You have no marketing team, so you are responsible for every aspect of your business, which means that vital marketing activities often do not happen. And when you do set aside time to take on those marketing tasks, you often get confused by the intricacies of the many marketing options that are available today. The decision about which of those options to use is in itself a complicated decision.

That is why I'm writing this book. As the CEO of different media companies, I have worked with small- and medium-size businesses for over thirty years. I've helped entrepreneurs understand their marketing needs through the countless changes in media and marketing over that time. From print to social media to emerging digital platforms, I've learned how a great marketing strategy can drive incredible business growth. This is a practical guide for small business owners who need to grow their customer base but don't know the basics of marketing for a small business. In this book, I outline a simple approach to marketing that any business owner can adapt to best reach their customers. This is a do-it-yourself guide to creating a small business marketing strategy—essential reading for business owners who find themselves flummoxed when it comes to reaching customers and building their business.

And please keep in mind that there is no need to read this book from the first page to the last. You can pick the chapters you are most interested in and which you think would be most valuable for your business in your current situation. You'll also notice that certain terms are bolded throughout—definitions of these terms are available at the back of the book in the "Terms to Know" section.

■　　■　　■

I was born in Oslo, Norway, in 1964 and studied at Oslo Business School, focusing on finance and marketing. Since 1987, I have worked in the local search industry with roles in IT, finance, operations, business development, sales, marketing and general/executive management. Because of this varied background, I have a 360-degree view of what needs to happen in a business and how the various parts of a business need to work together—and what happens when they don't work together!

Today, I am the CEO of FCR Media Group, which has offices in Estonia, the Czech Republic, Romania, Croatia, Belgium, and the Netherlands. I have lived in Oslo, Stockholm, Amsterdam, Tallinn, and Vienna and have also worked across Finland, Latvia, Lithuania, Slovakia, Hungary, Ireland, the Netherlands, and Uruguay. This background and my current activities have given me experience with many cultures, so I understand the universal problems that many businesses face.

FROM YELLOW PAGES TO WEB PAGES

At one point in my business life, I was involved in the first Yellow Pages available for the internet and for mobile phones. (At that time, they were not the same thing!) I am often asked why the Yellow Pages—which had been around for a long time and should have understood the importance of making it easy for people to find information—lost out to Google when it came to helping people find information online. My short answer is that the older, top management team members strongly believed in print publication and were not willing to make the changes and the investment (and take the profit risk) to aggressively pursue a digital solution. In fact, they didn't even see the *need* to do this at all because the print Yellow Pages was so well established and hugely profitable. That's why the first Online Yellow Pages were nothing but an implementation of the print version online. There were no special search functions and no additional information for the online user. Therefore, it is not surprising that more and more consumers preferred Google search to more conveniently get the kind of information that the Online Yellow Pages provided.

For this reason, Yellow Pages businesses are now a fraction of what they once were in terms of revenues and profit. They do still have strong core competencies and are now focused almost exclusively on digital solutions, but they were very late to the party and will never regain the dominant position in the market that they once enjoyed. Members of management were ignorant about what internet searching could become and were unwilling to invest the resources needed to become the leader in this new area. Even worse, many of the Yellow Pages publishers started to offer search engine products to their customers in order to somehow compensate for their losses in the search business. This way, they contributed to the success of search engines and further decreased the importance of their own search products.

> Small businesses do not have to let Amazon and other platforms take a huge cut of their revenue.

We see something similar happening to small businesses that are spending their money to market their products and services on Amazon and other global platforms—which is effectively giving those companies control over the future of their businesses. But it doesn't have to be that way. Small businesses do not have to let Amazon and other platforms take a huge cut of their revenue. You can have an online presence, get new customers, and service your new and existing customers better with your own digital solution combined with a physical location.

But of course, you have to put some thought into building your web shop. For example, consumers can get pretty disappointed with a web shop presenting pictures of goods that are not clickable and therefore do not provide any information a potential buyer would need to make a purchasing decision. We'll talk more specifically about professional web shops in chapter 6, but first, let's talk about the basics.

UNDERSTANDING THE BRAVE NEW WORLD OF COMMUNICATION TECHNOLOGY

These examples show that consumers are far more adept with new technologies and portals than their SMBs. As a consequence, they turn to US giants like Amazon to fulfill their needs, causing damage to their local economies. The only way out is for SMBs to understand the importance of today's communications technologies, explore them, and learn how to use them effectively. You need to realize that we live in an "instant" environment, where people's needs, desires, and demands are answered very quickly—and where they get impatient or give up if a business does not respond to them speedily. Businesses need to be more responsive today than they ever have before. This is no longer a "nice to have"; it's a requirement. Consumers have so many alternatives at their fingertips that they will quickly look elsewhere if your business is not responsive enough.

If you don't catch on to this, if you don't learn how to use the latest technology, you will be left in the dust. I've already told you about my experience with the top management of the Yellow Pages, about their refusal to recognize that a new technology, the internet, was here to stay. I had a similar experience with spreadsheets. In 1988, I prepared a business spreadsheet on one of the first spreadsheet apps for the CEO and the chairman of the company I was working for. They were so skeptical that a computer program could accurately compute spreadsheet data that they actually had someone check the spreadsheet stats with a calculator! This is the kind of skepticism about new technology that will sink a business in the digital age.

I also got the first Ericsson mobile phone when it came out. It was as big as a brick and cost the same as an iPhone costs today—but that was thirty years ago, so it was a lot more money than it is now. I mention this to make the point that I've always been a gadget freak and an early adopter. I get new technology as quickly as I can and work with it before a lot of people even have it—or, in some cases, even know it exists. This gives me early insight into how to use and take advantage of these new technologies and longer experience using them when they become generally accepted—and that's the kind of insight and experience I'll share with you in this book.

THE NEW NORMAL

There is a kind of willful ignorance being displayed right now, during the COVID pandemic, about what will happen with technology afterward. Far too many people actually believe that the tremendously increased use of digital solutions to communicate and do business will mostly go away after the pandemic is over. They think people will return to their old behavior and stop using digital solutions so much when life gets back to the pre-COVID normal. But things will never be the same again. Instead, we will have a *new* normal, where people continue to use digital solutions more than they ever did before. So it is crucial for all businesses to go digital to have a compelling internet presence—which means a presence that is clear, engaging, up-to-date, accurate, and appealing about the products and/or services the business is offering.

There are issues with digital businesses that are different from nondigital ones. For example, consumers change their habits more easily and frequently. Young people today consume very little regular, scheduled TV; instead, they find programs they want to watch online. Also, more and more people check ratings and reviews online before buying a product or service—whether they plan to buy it online or in a brick-and-mortar store.

Because of the ubiquity of online reviews, people can easily put out negative information about your business. The platforms that allow consumers to post those negative reviews won't counter them, so you need to keep track of them and be ready to counter those negative reviews yourself to answer any criticisms quickly and firmly. You can try to get an unfair review removed, but it is a very time-consuming process, and even if it is removed from one site, it might reappear on another. So you need to be vigilant.

To win in today's combination online/offline world, you should control your messaging, and you need to deliver the same messaging online as in your store or office. Potential customers need to learn what you are known for and what needs you cover, and that information should be easily accessible to them. The purpose of this book is to help you decide who you are—what your brand is—and how to ensure that your brand will be easily accessible to anyone who is interested in your products and/or services. And I am happy I can help you do this. Based on my broad experiences in marketing and management, and my expertise with the latest communication technology, I will describe in this book the basic marketing strategies and tools you need to get yourself and your business fit for the challenges of the new normal. And you *can* do it yourself. Let's get started.

CHAPTER ONE

WHAT AM I KNOWN FOR?

AN INTRODUCTION TO BRAND STRATEGY

■ ■ ■

While every baker sells bread, no two bakers sell exactly the same kind of bread. When establishing its brand, a bakeshop's first—and very important—job is to figure out how their baked goods are unique and what its customers love about those baked goods and about the experience of coming to the shop. The same need is there for any kind of small business. You need to understand what sets you apart, how you're currently presenting your business to your customers, how what you do impacts your customers. Only then can you present your business effectively to the world via the various platforms and technologies that are now available, which we will delve into in this book.

Can you define what your business does that is unique? Do you understand what you are known for now? Are you clear about what you would like to be known for going forward? In ancient Greece, "Know thyself" was one of the three maxims inscribed at the entrance to the Temple of Apollo at Delphi, where people went to have the

Delphic Oracle predict their future. It will be much easier to predict—and make happen—a positive future for your business if you know yourself and you know exactly what you have to offer potential customers that is different from what your competitors offer.

You need to understand what sets you apart.

You have to make it clear how what you offer will meet your customers' needs. The reality of who you are in the world is established by the perceptions people get from doing business with you. So talk to your customers, and find out what they like about doing business with you, what they get from you that keeps them coming back. If you're starting a new business, talk to the kinds of consumers who would be interested in what you want to offer and find out what they need and want from such a business. This knowledge should affect how you act like a businessperson. It should teach you how to present yourself clearly and with impact. It should teach you how you might adapt or expand your products and/or services to meet your customers' needs and how you talk to them.

THE IMPORTANCE OF BRAND

Having a coherent and synchronized brand is the essential first step toward increasing consumer awareness of your business through digital and other means. New business owners—or owners whose businesses want to increase their visibility—need to consider how they want to present themselves to consumers and convey that message in a clear, unified way. This includes several parts:

- **A compelling business name.** It needs to convey something about what you do, even if that's just obliquely, and be engaging enough to pique the public's interest.

- **An attractive logo.** Like your business name, it needs to say something compelling about your business and catch the public's eye. It is important to use one logo in the color(s) you define. Never use a logo in different colors or in an inverse version. You only have one logo, and this should be used everywhere.

- **A clear definition.** When defining how you want to be perceived by the public, make sure it complies with the real nature of your company. This means:

  - The company name, colors, design, and logo should be suitable to your offering and the target group you want to address.

  - Your style of writing and speaking is also an important part of your brand and can help you build your brand and be recognized.

  - All of these elements have to be tailor-made for your offering and your **buyer personas.** For example, a funeral home certainly has different requirements than a florist shop. A jeans shop for young people will use a different language than a consultant for big investments.

  - The way you present yourself should not imply promises you cannot fulfill. For example, a restaurant pretending to be a five-star gourmet temple but offering typical homemade cooking in a modest environment will not be very successful.

  - The way you want to appear in your market should be the guideline for your and your employees' daily activities. It should be congruent with your corporate identity and lived day after day by you and your staff.

- **A style guide.** You also should have a style guide for developing your brand's unique appearance and voice. This is necessary for your **website**, letters to your customers, folders, brochures, coupons—in short, for all of your corporate communication. Working out a style guide by defining all the elements mentioned above will help you and your staff to work out a consistent appearance and verbal style for all communication channels.

- **A clearly stated purpose.** You need to convey in clear and strong terms what you offer potential customers and what is unique about what you offer. Describe your USP—unique selling proposition!

- **A compelling list of products and/or services.** People won't come to you if they don't know exactly what you can provide them or do for them.

- **High-quality products and services.** The quality of your product or service will convince customers to come back to you and is the basic requirement to create customer loyalty. If this is provided, customers will trust in you and your offerings. They will return, make purchases again and again, and recommend your products and services to their friends and other people. So you should *never* stop thinking about how you can improve your offering—and you should motivate your staff to do the same.

- **Consistent presentation.** Present your business on your **website**, in print or digital ads, in person, or wherever you publicize it in a simple, direct, consistent way that people will begin to recognize and respond to.

The business school will call all of this brand management, but if that seems too pretentious for your small business, just think of it as having a clear and consistent way of presenting yourself—which is something that we all want from each other, professionally and personally. Doing this can have a real impact on how consumers perceive your business.

For example, my favorite bakery managed to find the perfect way to address its target group. Of course, they sell excellent products—that's a basic requirement. But additionally, they composed a great market presence—consistent from the name of the company and its products to the logo to the carryout bags and interior design of the bakery shops. In times when supermarkets offer all kinds of bakery goods at discount prices, they are able to get their customers queuing up to buy their bread at a very high price. This example demonstrates that putting some effort into the quality of products combined with designing a consistent market appearance really pays off. And this is not only necessary for big companies but for each SMB as well.

NO WORRIES

Having managed local search companies, set directions, and managed alignments for many organizations, I can help you do this. My expertise is in getting organizations to develop a real customer focus, a real understanding of their customers' needs and wants.

My current company partners with Facebook, Google, and other media platforms, so I understand how such communications platforms work from the inside and will advise you on how best to use them for your purposes.

So do not miss the train—jump on it *now*, before it leaves the station for good! Relying on my extensive digital knowledge and experience, an important part of what I do is advising businesses about what they need to do to get on board via digital communication and marketing and stay competitive in a business world that is increasingly digital. This book will go a long way toward helping you do the same.

KEY TAKEAWAYS

- In order to present your business to the world effectively, you first need to understand what sets you apart, how you're currently presenting your business to your customers, and how what you do impacts your customers.

- Talk to your current customers to find out what they like about doing business with you, what they get from you that keeps them coming back. Or if you're starting a new business, talk to the kinds of consumers who would be interested in what you want to offer and find out what they need and want from such a business.

- You need to understand that we live in an "instant" environment, where you should know people's needs, desires, and demands very quickly.

- To present what you do that is unique to consumers and convey that message in a clear, unified way, you need

  - a clearly stated definition and purpose;
  - a compelling business name and logo;
  - a presentation of your company that complies with the real nature of your offering;
  - promises that you can fulfill;
  - a compelling list of products and/or services meeting high-quality standards; and
  - clear and consistent presentation on all communication channels, including design, colors, voice— preferably presented in a style guide that ensures consistency.

- If you don't learn how to use the latest technology to serve your customers, you will be left in the dust.

CHAPTER TWO

WHO ARE MY CUSTOMERS?

UNDERSTANDING YOUR CLIENTS' NEEDS

■   ■   ■

Most larger companies have what's called a customer relationship management (CRM) system that tracks and stores information about customer purchases and about customers themselves. The CRM profiles tell them who their customers are, where they live, how they became customers, what they need and want, how they like to be approached, what their buying habits are, what their estimated household income is, and so on. Such information provides the basis for targeted marketing that is much more likely to be successful than general marketing efforts. Unfortunately, most small businesses do not have CRM systems. But if small businesses want to be successful today, it is essential that they understand who their customers are.

As people become more and more digitally oriented, as the consumer gets used to digital solutions, small businesses need to follow them there, or those consumers will start to buy from businesses that *will* serve them online. So first of all, you need to know where your customers "are," technologically speaking, and be able to reach them there. Most online businesses also store customers' purchase and personal data, and they use this data to market more effectively. As a small business owner, you cannot afford to cede this advantage to businesses that know and track their customers better than you do. Even if today you think you know all your customers and what they are buying from you, you might be missing out on *what else* they might buy from you if you knew them and their habits better.

> If small businesses want to be successful today, it is essential that they understand who their customers are.

My wife is a good example. She will buy most of her groceries at one store but buys her fruit and vegetables at another store—even though the first store has the same fruit and vegetables—because she thinks the fruit and vegetables are better at the second store. If the first store knew this about her, they could appeal to her by convincing her of the quality of their own fruits and vegetables and by touting the convenience of only having to shop at one grocery store.

For another example, if you're a handyman and keep track of the work you do for each customer, when a customer calls again to have something done, you can refer to your notes and discuss what you did for the customer previously. Most customers would be impressed that you recalled specific details about what you did for them previously, which makes a personal connection and displays your professionalism.

The key is to get to know your customers, find out their needs, and deliver extras based on your knowledge about them. The goal of doing this is to serve your customers better than they expect to be served, so they have a positive experience, want to continue to do business with you, and recommend you to family and friends.

Is it difficult to do this? No, but it does require some discipline, putting in the time and effort in the midst of everything else you have to do to run a small business. You will need to start collecting customer data in a structured way. It's best to have a system that is easy to use and enables you to analyze your customers' data.

MY SPECIAL ADVICE

When you decide to buy a CRM system, I advise you to choose a system that collects all your customer data for specific situations in a central location. This way, you can get a 360-degree view of your customer and trigger certain processes for related customer groups.

STEERING MARKETING CAMPAIGNS

Using your CRM software, you can send information about your products and services to those customers who could be highly interested, meaning that it speaks the language of this group and arrives at the right time for them. For example, being a landscaper, you can select those customers known for having a house with a garden and mail them an offer for planting plants or grass in the spring and pruning their plants and trees in the fall. If you have customers you know who live in apartments with balconies, you can offer them smaller plants and pots.

OPPORTUNITY MANAGEMENT

The CRM data can also show you which customer groups to approach first about acquiring additional products and services. Getting back to our landscaper example, the landscaper could select customers known to buy new plants and use pruning services regularly because they are more likely to be open to new products and services.

ORDER-MANAGEMENT AND CUSTOMER SERVICE

By storing customer data in a central location, you can more easily and quickly send appropriate offers. And when a customer calls, you can easily call up that customer's data and the history of your relationship and have it right in front of you as you speak with the customer, ensuring that you handle the call in a highly professional manner.

WIN-BACK OPPORTUNITY

Of course, the CRM data also tells you if a customer *has not* bought your goods for quite some time. Being aware of this, you can reach out to this customer and make a special offer designed to win them back.[1]

---

1   There are a lot of CRM systems to choose from. Capterra is an excellent resource for reviewing and deciding between many different CRM systems. Visit their interactive list "Best CRM Software for Small Businesses" at https://www.capterra.com/customer-relationship-management-software/s/small-businesses/. You should be able to find a CRM system on this big list that will fit your needs. I can highly recommend the CRM system my own company offers: Sitee.io.

If you don't want to immediately invest in a CRM system, you can begin by writing down customer information or typing it into a document on your computer—the important thing is to get started, to try it out. Here is an example of how you might begin to collect customer information: When a new customer comes in or gets in touch, ask how they found out about you and why they chose to do business with you and record that information. That way, you can start to learn about where your new customers are coming from and why they're coming—which will teach you what your strengths are, what appeals to consumers about your business. It's really quite easy to take a step like this because it costs you nothing, and you'll learn something about where and how to attract new customers.

Another relatively easy step is to track the effects of your marketing campaigns. For example, you can code a couple of different kinds of direct mail pieces so that when someone responds to it, you'll know which piece they are responding to. That way, you can track the effects of your marketing spending and find out what approach is most effective at getting people interested in your business.

The proprietor of my local pizzeria has learned my habits. The last time I ate in there, he told me that on the following Tuesday, they would have lasagna on the takeaway menu. He did this in a very low-key way, just passing on information he knew would interest me because he knows that when he has lasagna on the menu, my son and I often order it. This didn't feel pushy at all; it felt like good customer service because he knows what we like. The pizzeria does not have a system to track this; the proprietor just has the information in his head. And that makes me wonder how many more lasagnas he could sell if he sent an email about the Tuesday special to all of his customers who he knows like lasagna. Knowing your customers makes it much easier to sell to them repeatedly.

BEWARE OF DATA PRIVACY RULES

After you try out collecting data manually and begin to see its value, you will be ready to start working with a CRM system tailored for small businesses. Bear in mind, though, that when you collect data from customers, you *must* have them sign a consent agreement, where they agree to let you store certain data about them and use it only in certain ways, which has to be spelled out in the agreement. There are a number of ready-made agreements of this kind available, which you can ask your customers to sign. To be on the safe side, you can, of course, also consult

> When you collect data from customers, you must have them sign a consent agreement.

your lawyer. Considering the current privacy rules in Europe, it is essential that you get your clients' consent and store the consent form properly. The fines for storing private data improperly and/or without permission are large, and they will increase over time because this is increasingly becoming a significant issue for government and private consumer protection organizations.

When you have this consent, you can gather, store, and track personal data such as gender, age, contact information, preferences, needs, buying habits (so you learn what the customers usually buy from you and offer related products or services)—even the customers' birthdays, which you use to send special birthday offers. You should also get your customers' consent to receiving email, direct mail, and maybe even text messages from you—whichever forms of communication they're comfortable with.

BUILDING CUSTOMER PERSONAS

Besides storing the data of your actual customers concerning their contact data, purchases, etc., it is recommended that you also build out what's known as **buyer or customer personas**. This is not about gathering real data but about developing a picture of typical customers based on information collected while doing business with all of your customers and prospects. It is a generalized representation of your average customer. The **customer personas** enable you to target your broadest marketing and customer acquisition efforts, where you're casting a wide net but want to capture the kind of customers that are most likely to appreciate what you offer.

The kind of information you should consider to establish your **customer/buyer personas** includes the following.

For individual customers:

- Gender

- Family status (Single? Married? Kids?)

- Residence

- Nationality

- Education

- Employment/profession

- Estimated income

- Social status (Middle class? Upper class?)

- Hobbies

- Media consumed most often

- Goals and values

- Possible motivation to buy or not to buy your products and services

- What it's important to do in order to keep them as a customer

For business customers:

- Position in the company

- Location

- Industry segment

- Products and services they buy or sell

- Number of employees

- Revenue and market share

- Importer and/or exporter?

- How long in business (Start-up or company with long tradition?)

- Goals and values

- Possible motivation to buy or not to buy your products

- What it's important to do in order to keep them as a customer

Based on these considerations, you will be able to draw two to three **buyer/customer personas** that characterize your customer base. In order to make these personas more tangible, you can even give them a name and a personality. For example, Buyer/Customer Persona One is called Jack Generous. He is single, has no kids, and lives nearby in a fancy apartment. He has an above-average income and is more focused on quality and what's new than on price. Buyer/Customer Persona Two is called Mary Pennypincher. She is married, has two kids, and works part time. With a limited budget, she is very focused on saving and buying cheap. When a customer enters your store who identifies with the Mary Pennypincher persona, you will realize: "Ah, here comes Mary Pennypincher. Time to bring out the coupons and special offers." When, on the other hand, someone comes along who is more in line with Jack Generous, then you better show your newest and highest-priced products. With the help of these personas in your mind, you will know how to respond to each customer and treat them in such a way that they will leave your store or office a satisfied customer. And they will be much more likely to come back because they were happy with the tailor-made treatment and product/service offers you provided.

It is better to serve a small, well-defined customer group in the best possible way than to try to address a mass market. Don't play "Jack of all trades and master of none," but consciously limit yourself to your market niche and your target group.

A NOTE ABOUT CASE STUDIES

I have promised to give you as much practical advice as possible in this book on how to make your business more successful using digital marketing. This includes describing real projects that my company, FCR Media, and our subsidiary, DexVille, have implemented for our clients that show digital marketing solutions in action. These case studies will be interspersed throughout the book.

CASE STUDY:
MUSKLE (ROVAN SPORTS)

Knowing your customer is essential to build a strong brand and a solid ground for your business. The following DexVille case shows the importance of defining your **buyer personas** before defining your brand.

THE COMPANY

Rovan Sports has specialized in personal coaching of athletes for more than twenty years. They sell sports and diet food, give sports advice, and make tailor-made nutrition plans.

THE CHALLENGE

Rovan Sports initially contacted DexVille to integrate their brand portfolio of four companies into a single brand that would stand out strongly in a growing market. After the rebranding, Rovan asked DexVille to build a website and promote the new brand.

THE SOLUTION

DexVille set up a brand identity workshop to analyze the four brands with the client, asking questions such as: What do the different brands stand for? Do they overlap? And what do the customer target groups for each brand look like?

DexVille then defined four **buyer personas** with growth potential and showed the client that their current positioning only appealed to two of these four personas. DexVille designed a new MUSKLE logo to unite all four segments of the company, developed a brand book, and applied this in all of Rovan's communication channels.

DexVille next built a modern e-commerce store with good **SEO** traction that seamlessly combined all elements of the new corporate identity and presented a user experience that made it easy for consumers to find the right products. This **website** included colorful images in natural environments, dynamic animations, and fresh motivational copy that appealed to the target groups of fitness enthusiasts. DexVille created e-commerce campaigns dedicated to sending traffic to this new site.

THE RESULT

The dedicated e-commerce campaigns are producing high conversion rates, with Facebook Dynamic Ads performing best so far.

CROSS-SELLING

So step one is to store data about your customers in a system. Step two is to study that data and figure out what suitable offers you could make to customers on a regular basis. Step three is to find a gentle way to communicate this to your customers so they see it as a positive service rather than a pushy attempt to sell them more. Keep in mind that we are all consumers, and we all have a strong tendency to buy from the same places and buy the same products or services from those places. It's also much less expensive to serve existing customers than it is to find new ones. Knowledge about your customers makes it much easier to influence their choices, to adjust your ads and your offers to the needs and wants of individuals or groups. If you know a customer likes lasagna, you can let them know it's available. If you know a customer is vegetarian, you'll make a good impression if you highlight vegetable dishes and a bad impression if you push meat or seafood dishes. If you know a customer has dietary restrictions for health reasons, you can recommend dishes that take that into account.

To give some examples from other small businesses:

- A car salesman who knows that a customer he's sold to likes hybrid cars can let them know each time the newest model comes in, telling them about the new features that the latest model has.

- A bookseller who knows a customer's reading tastes can recommend newly arrived books that suit the customer's interests.

If you make such recommendations gently—in other words, in a way that emphasizes the benefits to the customer—they will be seen as a service, not as an unwanted sales pitch. The world is becoming more and more digital. Storing and analyzing customer data has gotten much easier and less expensive for small businesses. This means that more and more businesses will do it, which means that you ought to be doing it to stay competitive.

It is also possible to use technology for just certain areas of customer service. For example, one of my customers uses Sitee.io, a CRM tool, daily to handle support inquiries. It allows the company to field support calls, issue "tickets" describing customer problems that need to be solved, make appointments with customers, and so on. The customers love it because they have someone to ask about problems, and the company responds to their queries about those problems.

It is this kind of personalized service—only possible if you go to the trouble of understanding your customers' needs—that will help your small business fend off the competition and grow.

KEY TAKEAWAYS

- Study your customer base—start simple on paper, and then go digital!

- Using CRM systems will help in setting up a customer database storing your customers' preferences and allow cross-selling.

- Always be aware of data privacy rules!

- Develop two to three **buyer/customer personas** you want to focus on!

- Less is more: Don't play "Jack of all trades and achieving nothing." Being precise in defining your buyer/customer profiles will help you to develop unique products and services.

- Be aware of your customers' needs and expectations; try to deliver the little extra based on your knowledge about them!

CHAPTER THREE

HOW DO I SERVE MY CUSTOMERS?

TALKING ABOUT YOUR SERVICE

■ ■ ■

Once you really know what your story is as a company and who your customers and potential customers are, you should understand how your products or services are meeting your customers' needs. And you have to remain agile, so if your customers' needs and desires change, you can adapt to those changes. For example, an electrician today could be keeping up with what's happening in the area of smart homes and offering the latest products and services for such homes. And a baker, due to the increased awareness of the problems caused by gluten, could offer some gluten-free breads and pastries. A technology store with young customers highly interested in adopting new technology could highlight the latest products for them as soon as they came in, using a text message or an email.

What you offer needs to align with how you want people to perceive your business. The European airline Ryanair is not likely to attract people who like to be pampered when they travel, with its bare-bones service, where virtually every "extra," from water to a pillow, costs extra. But for bargain hunters who just want to get from place A to place B and are willing to forgo snacks and drinks for cheap airfare, the way Ryanair presents itself is ideal. How they present themselves matches what they deliver—and you should do the same with your business.

> What you offer needs to align with how you want people to perceive your business.

Certainly, Ryanair researched the European travel market and found that there were enough people who just wanted to get where they were going cheaply and built an airline on that basis. Do you know what your potential and existing customers want? If not, ask them! You can do it casually in conversation, or you can ask them to answer a few questions or survey and give them a small reward for doing so. It will be worth the investment, which, in any case, does not have to be large.

It's also highly important to constantly screen the market and learn what your competitors are up to. Search engines are a simple way to do this. Take your time and check out which products and services your competitors are offering and what kind of prices they are charging for products and services similar to your own. Based on these insights and knowing your buyers, work out a unique selling proposition (USP) for your company, the reason why consumers will buy your products and services rather than those of your competitors. Competitive research will enable you to design a product and service portfolio that is unique in the market and offers a clear advantage to your customers.

Note that you should take into account how much your customers are willing to pay and how much you need to make to cover your costs.

The price should be part of your overall market presence and business strategy: Do you want to offer high-quality, luxurious products and services at a relatively high price, or are you aiming for best-priced offerings? As the bakery example above demonstrates, pricing is part of the USP.

EXCEEDING CUSTOMER EXPECTATIONS

But beyond the basics of what your customers want, you can also provide extras that will set your business apart. For example, an Italian restaurant could give its patrons a complimentary grappa or small dessert at the end of the meal. And if most hairdressers were offering their patrons basic coffee and water, a salon could install an espresso machine and provide pastries to go with this higher-end coffee, making its patrons feel appreciated and special. A taxi service could offer discounted services to elderly people to get them to medical appointments and to run errands. A bakery could emphasize its use of great traditional methods of baking handed down through the generations to achieve extraordinary breads and pastries.

After meeting your customers' basic needs—the needs they expect you to satisfy—the key to cementing their loyalty is to *exceed* their expectations. This is when it is crucial to know who specifically your customer is so that you can effectively exceed their expectations and make them repeat customers. Going above and beyond isn't possible if you don't have some sort of CRM-like system (even if it's just notes you take) to tell you who your individual buyers are and what "above and beyond" would look like for each of them. If you treat your customers well, they will not only come back but also will recommend your business to family and friends.

Exceeding expectations should happen both of these ways:

- Your basic products and/or services should be good enough to impress your customers and to set you apart from—or at least put you on the same level with—the very best vendors of such products and/or services. This starts, of course, with actually providing the best products and services you can. Then, strategies such as responding quickly, matching competitors' prices, guaranteeing the work, giving payment back without question if the customer isn't satisfied, and so on can help establish your business as belonging in the category of best vendors. One of the reasons Amazon is so successful in convincing people to order online is that they make it as easy as possible for customers to return products. And in my own company, I insist that employees get back to any customer who has called with a question or problem within two hours—and customers notice this responsiveness.

- You should find ways to do something extra for your customers that will cement your business in their minds and motivate them to recommend it to others. It doesn't have to be something big, just something thoughtful, such as a free entrée or dessert from a restaurant on a customer's birthday, a limousine ride to work when a car is dropped off at a repair shop, or a package of energy-saving light bulbs from an electrician. And the more the "extra" aligns with the products or services you provide, the clearer the impression of your business will be in the customer's mind.

This approach will establish and maintain your reputation as a great company to do business with.

There are actually six steps in the process of exceeding expectations:

1. Set customer expectations by communicating clearly—in ads, signage, direct mail, or whatever tools you use to make consumers aware of your business—what it is you do and how you do it.

2. Respond as quickly as possible when consumers reach out to you for information or help—answer the phone within a few rings, call people back within twenty-four hours—and be as helpful as you can be when you speak to them.

3. Once you've set the right expectations in your communications, deliver on those expectations.

4. Sell customers what they feel they need, not what you want them to buy. You should, of course, guide customers to what you think are the products or services that will best serve their needs, differentiating between different products and services by pointing out their individual features. But sometimes customers make strange choices, and in the end, you should give them what they want.

5. Provide that extra something. It makes your business memorable and establishes a connection between you and your customers.

6. When customers complain, remain friendly with them, and offer them a fair, reasonable solution to their problem.

Another important strategy for establishing and maintaining a good reputation is keeping tabs on online reviews and responding to them. It's obviously important to tell your side of the story in response to a negative review—and you need to do that without being insulting to the customer, no matter how angry they may have made you. Focus on the complaint, not the complainer, so readers will see that you are respectful and responsive. Make it clear that you're truly listening to the customer, being empathetic. But you also have to counter the complaint, so readers of the review will see your point of view and see that you really tried to be responsive. With smaller issues, it's probably easier in the end to just give the customer what they want, to offer a reasonable solution to the problem they encountered. A few people may take advantage of this, but it's much better than having an extended conflict with a customer—especially in a public forum. We'll touch more on ratings and reviews in chapter 8.

> Another important strategy for establishing and maintaining a good reputation is keeping tabs on online reviews and responding to them.

Set customer expectations, live up to those expectations—and whenever possible, exceed them by providing something extra—and make amends when a customer feels you have not lived up to their expectations. These are key steps in establishing and maintaining a successful small business.

KEY TAKEAWAYS

- Once you really know what your story is as a company and who your customers and potential customers are, you should understand how your products or services are meeting your customers' needs.

- Do you know what your potential and existing customers want? If not, ask them!

- Analysis of your market and competition analysis will enable you to create a unique selling proposition and a competitive pricing policy.

- Your basic products and/or services should be good enough to impress your customers and to set you apart from—or at least put you on the same level with—the very best vendors of such products and/or services.

- You should also find ways to do something extra for your customers that will cement your business in their minds and motivate them to recommend it to others.

- There are six steps to exceeding customer expectations:

   1. Set customer expectations by communicating clearly what your business does and how you do it.

2. Respond as quickly as possible when consumers reach out to you for information or help.

3. Once you've set expectations, deliver on them.

4. Sell customers what they feel they need, not what you want them to buy.

5. Provide something extra.

6. When customers complain, be friendly and offer them a fair solution.

- Keep tabs on online reviews of your business and respond to them, whether they are negative or positive.

CHAPTER FOUR

DO I NEED A WEBSITE?

THE BASIS FOR AN EFFICIENT DIGITAL PRESENCE

■ ■ ■

After COVID-19 hit the world, it was not really a question anymore whether or not a business needed an online presence—or, at least, it shouldn't have been. Lockdowns, home offices, social distancing, quarantining, and so on suddenly changed life as we had known it. In order to survive, companies were, and still are, adapting to the new rules of doing business. Without face-to-face customer interactions or physical presence, they had to quickly find new ways to deal with their customers. A professional **website**, including an online shop for people selling things directly, became a basic instrument for staying in business. Companies that didn't have a website had to quickly get one—or pay the price. And those that already had one had to make sure their site was up to date and really met the requirements of a professional digital presence. Those who had a really good website, including a store when appropriate, even before the pandemic, were the lucky and successful ones.

For those who are finally realizing that they need a professional website, there are three different ways to go about building a website for your business:

- Do It Yourself (DIY)

- Do It for Me (DIFM)

- Do It with Me (DIWM)

I will describe the advantages and disadvantages of each of these approaches below.

DO IT YOURSELF (DIY)

There are quite a few excellent tools to enable you to create your own website if you're willing to put in the time and effort. Though many website-building tools make it as simple as possible, it still requires a lot of thought and learning to bring it off. But it can be done!

Pros: This is, of course, by far the least expensive way to develop a website, and these website building tools make it relatively easy to make changes to your website quickly without having to consult with someone else or waiting for them to do it. There are thousands of templates for the overall design of a website, even for digital shops. For example, in Belgium, we recommend www.wix.com, which offers a variety of designs for creating an online presence and selling online.

Cons: This is the most time-consuming approach, of course, and there is the danger that you might end up with something less professional than you want, with inferior functionality and poor capabilities, and not optimized for **search engine optimization (SEO)**, which we'll talk about here in just a minute. You might also run into extra costs for additional functions or templates you had not foreseen. Finally, you could face technical challenges that you're unable to personally overcome, although most website design vendors provide *some* level of support.

DO IT FOR ME (DIFM)

There are many experienced website designers and publishers that can take much of the work out of your hands—although you will still have to make decisions about the design and content you want them to execute.

Pros: Provided you have chosen a good, professional individual or agency, you can rest assured your site will look and function in a highly professional manner and will be optimized for **SEO**. It will include capabilities that support your business and will leave you more time to run your business—the time you would otherwise have spent on building your website.

Cons: The biggest disadvantage of this approach is its cost. This is the most expensive approach—although the investment is likely to pay off—and it will probably take more time to make changes than it would if you could immediately make the changes yourself. You also have to be very organized and clear about what you have in mind when briefing the people who will work on the website, so you don't end up with something you don't want.

There are many experienced website designers and publishers that can take much of the work out of your hands—although you will still have to make decisions about the design and content you want them to execute.

DO IT WITH ME (DIWM)

This approach is a hybrid of the first two approaches, which means it can turn out to be the best of both worlds, but it can also introduce the problems of both worlds.

Pros: You will get a professional website with good technical performance that is optimized for search engines at a somewhat lower cost than the DIFM approach. You will also be involved in the design process to a greater extent than in the DIFM approach. Finally, you can save money by setting up the website so you can do your own updates of content and certain design changes.

Cons: The cost is higher than the DIY approach, and it's more time consuming than the DIFM approach.

Whether you choose DIFM or DIWM, it is worth looking for a provider especially suitable for SMBs willing to take care of your special needs concerning price and product.

WEBSITE HOSTING

Regardless of the approach you decide to take, you will need to pay a website hosting service to store your website, make it available on the internet, and provide a domain with an email address—and ensure that it *stays* available online. If you are choosing a DIFM or a DIWM website, your provider will take care of hosting your website. Make sure the website hosting service your builder is providing or you use offers the following services:

- High uptime

- Sufficient web space

- A twenty-four-seven support hotline that you can access online, via phone, or through live chat

- A fast website loading speed

- Excellent security and protection from spam and malware (enabling **HTTPS**)

- Daily backups that save your content

- Clear privacy and **cookie** use policies

- Web stats about visitors and usage

There are many web-hosting services, among them IONOS, HostEurope, webgo, and raidboxes.

ABOUT SEO AND MAKING YOUR WEBSITE ACCESSIBLE

Most consumers start their searches for products and services on search engines like Google. Studies show that only search results that get listed on top of the first page are considered by most searchers to be worthy of a closer look.[2] There is a saying that goes: "There is no better place to hide a dead body than on page two of Google search results." Therefore it is a must for your website to be constructed and filled with content in such a way that it scores as high as possible in search results and ends up high on the first page of search results. The goal should be to rank among the top three search results. This ensures that when consumers search for your products and services, they will find you before they find your competitor.

The mechanism for achieving this is called **search engine optimization (SEO)**. Using **SEO** techniques makes sure that your website is listed in a top position on a search results page. Search engines want to offer great, useful, trustworthy search results to their users.

---

2   Johannes Beus, "Click Probabilities in Google SERPS," 2015, accessed September 2021, https://www.sistrix.de/news/klickwahrscheinlichkeiten-in-den-google-serps/.

Therefore, all the elements important for a great user experience play into **SEO** and a higher ranking, including the following:

- Good content that includes the kind of terms (**keywords**) that consumers are searching with

- Shared content from—and **links** to—other websites

- A rapid website loading time

- Great usability on all devices

HAVING GOOD CONTENT

If you know your customers' and prospects' profiles (see chapter 2) and their pain points, you will be able to publish on your website exactly the kind of content they're looking for. As a consequence, your website will be used often and even shared with others. This will enable search engines to recognize that your site is trustworthy and of interest to users, which will improve its search ranking, so it appears higher in search results.

> It is important to include keywords that characterize what you want to be found for.

Additionally, it is important to include **keywords** that characterize what you want to be found for. Consider carefully which **keywords**, terms, or even questions a consumer is likely to use when searching for products and services like yours. These **keywords**, terms, and questions should be included on your website. And, of course, these **keywords** need to be used in the context of good, usable content on these topics. If yours is a local shop serving a particular neighborhood, this should also be highlighted on your website because consumers often search by locals for convenience.

You should not use **SEO** blindly but in the context of providing good and useful content helping your customers and prospects to solve their problems. Good content requires constant updates. If you run a store, you need to regularly check your stock and renew the merchandise on your shelves and in your shop windows. The same is true for your website. It, too, should be continually refreshed to keep it interesting—and to keep it high in search results.

To sum up, in the words of the world's most popular search engine, Google's Search Quality Evaluator Guidelines report from October 2020[3], important factors for a Page Quality rating are EAT: expertise, authoritativeness, and trustworthiness:

Expertise: You have to prove you have the expertise to talk about certain topics—particularly in the case of YMYL (your money, your life):

- Show your company, your education, your trainings

- Constantly update the content of your site

Authoritativeness: You have a reputation in the field; others can build your authority by linking to your website and sharing your content, such as blog posts, case studies, testimonials, and reviews.

Trustworthiness: You have to prove your legitimacy and maintain the transparency and accuracy of the website and its content. Be aware of all legal requirements regarding the following:

- Legal disclosure concerning your company name, address, contact data, registered company number

- Data protection statement

- **Cookie** information

---

3   "Search Quality Evaluator Guidelines," October 14, 2020, accessed September 2021, https://static.googleusercontent.com/media/guidelines.raterhub.com/de//searchqualityevaluatorguidelines.pdf.

SHARING AND LINKING

Good, authentic content is popular among consumers. Your having shared content and **links** to other sites—as well as people linking to your site—demonstrates to search engines that your site is authoritative and popular and thus should be ranked high in search results. Some companies try to get as many **links** as possible on their pages, actively engaging in **link** building. But you need to be aware that quality is far better than quantity. Too many low-quality **links** are rated as spam by search engines and will cause your site to be ranked *lower* in search results.

Nevertheless, sites with a lot of **backlinks** rank above sites that don't have as many. You should definitely include **links** to **subpages** of *your own* website as well as to other sites. To get other websites to **link** to yours, you should provide content that people will want to refer to—for example, intriguing infographics and interesting reviews of the latest publications or reports about what's happening in your industry. Linking your website to your social media profiles is also an important step to take as a marketing tool. **SEO** expert Brian Dean conducted extensive research regarding the importance of **backlinks** and found that the number one results in Google searches have an average of 3.8 times more **backlinks** than the results in positions two to ten.[4] Additionally, getting **backlinks** from multiple different sites appears to be important for **SEO**. The number of domains linking to a site also has a positive correlation with the height of the ranking.

MAKING SURE YOUR WEBSITE LOADS QUICKLY

The time it takes to load a website is crucial when consumers are looking for a product or service. If it takes too long, they simply

---

4   Brian Dean, "We Analyzed 11.8 Million Google Search Results: Here's What We Learned About SEO," BackLinkO, April 28, 2020, accessed September 2021, https://backlinko.com/search-engine-ranking.

abandon the page and go on to the next site in their search results. The longer it takes to load the site, the faster the **bounce rate** increases. Various studies show that loading times should not exceed three seconds. The load time for mobile sites should be even shorter, taking no longer than between one to two seconds.[5]

Slow loading times can have a negative impact on your **SEO** ranking and make a negative impression on a consumer. If your page loads too slowly for the consumer to browse, it is very likely you won't get a second chance to win this person as a customer.

Google especially puts an emphasis on the user experience, and their Web Vital Report, published in spring 2021, has defined some factors such as Largest Contentful Paint (LCP), First Input Delay (FID), and Cumulative Layout Shift (CLS) as being essential for a good user experience.[6] Since these are highly technical, I suggest you ask your website provider or designer whether Google's Web Vitals have been taken into account.

USING MOBILE OPTIMIZATION AND/ OR RESPONSIVE DESIGN

More than half of website traffic comes from mobile devices.[7] Therefore, mobile optimization is key to keeping consumers happy.

5   MachMetrics Speed Blog, "Average Page Load Times for 2020: Are you faster?" December 21, 2019, accessed September 2021, https://www.machmetrics.com/ speed-blog/average-page-load-times-for-2020/.

6   Prashant Shukla, "Core Web Vitals: Definition, Introduction to LCP, FID & CLS, and Core Web Vitals Optimization Tips," Techmagnate, March 17, 2021, accessed September 2021, https://www.techmagnate.com/blog/google-core-web-vitals/; Core Web Vitals report - Search Console Help (google.com).

7   Simon Kemp, "Digital 2021 April Global Statshot Report," DataReportal, April 21, 2021, accessed September 2021, https://datareportal.com/reports/ digital-2021-april-global-statshot?rq=voice%20search.

Responsive design is even better because it means that a website is adapted to *all* devices: laptops, tablets, and mobile phones. With responsive design, content, pictures, and other elements can be seen and used effectively on any device without any restrictions. Mobile optimization and responsive design are key to a good user experience, and they are also beneficial for higher **SEO** rankings. Google and other search engines want their users to get relevant, high-quality search results that are optimized for the users' devices, so they rank websites with those qualities higher.

MY SPECIAL ADVICE

If you are developing a new website, I strongly recommend a responsive design site that automatically adapts to all devices. The advantages compared to a simply mobile-optimized site are obvious:

- You don't need to develop a mobile site specially designed for mobile devices with a special header and special content.

- You'll have just one website and one URL, saving you the effort of maintaining and updating two sites, and consumers won't be confused by your having two URLs for your site.

CASE STUDY:
MARSHALLS

The website is the focus of a digital presence. This DexVille case demonstrates that a professional website in combination with the right digital communication campaign can bring immediate success.

THE COMPANY

Marshalls (BE) is a leading supplier of tiles and pavers for terraces, driveways, and swimming pools. The company is continuously developing new and better products, using the best raw materials available.

THE CHALLENGE

After first rolling out a successful strategy to generate high-quality prospects with the help of a dedicated landing page, including a downloadable brochure, Marshalls asked DexVille to build a new digital communication campaign to further expand Marshalls' customer base, especially in the B2C market.

THE SOLUTION

DexVille built a new website with a strong focus on B2C, including access to the existing web shop, the best technical practices for **SEO** optimization, the right searchable content, and inspiring visuals that met the highest standards of digital design. The traffic generation strategy employed a mix of digital channels: **search engine advertising (SEA)**, **search engine optimization (SEO)**, and paid social ads. To respect the **customer journey** of each persona, the site offered microconversions (such as downloading the brochure) and macroconversions, such as visiting a product page or buying a product.

THE RESULT

The B2C website and traffic generation strategies generated 2,500 leads in four months, with a 15 percent conversion rate.

TECHNICAL FACTORS

Besides engaging, authentic, and frequently used content, search engines require special elements to be able to "read" a site well and to recognize how the content and the **keywords** are being used. Therefore, titles and descriptions are essential for building a website optimized for search engines. Missing those elements or having duplicate ones will lower the ranking of a site.

Additionally, be sure to name the files of the pictures you are displaying on your website, so they can be found by search engines. These elements need a speaking title and a short description. For example, naming a picture "IMG.2675.pdf" does not say anything and will not help the search engine to know what is featured. It is better to go for a title saying what the picture shows, such as "Lawnmower all-electric." Additionally, it is recommended to describe the picture in more detail— for example, "Stand-on mower hydro-powered."

A site map with a structured overview of the documents on the website tells a search engine what is most important on your site, so developing a site map with a clear and accurate overview of content/pages as well as updates is essential to ensuring that your content is quickly and correctly indexed by search engines.

THE IMPORTANCE OF SECURITY

Search engines not only want to offer useful and authentic content to their users, but they also want to protect their users by sending them to secure sites. Installing an **SSL (secure socket layer)** certificate and building an **HTTPS (hypertext transfer protocol secure)**-enabled website is an easy and very efficient way to secure safe data transfer, so sites that do this are ranked higher than ones that don't. This approach protects sensitive information such as usernames and passwords, which makes consumers more confident about using a site.

ACHIEVING BARRIER-FREE ACCESSIBILITY

Your website should also be accessible for people with limitations in their seeing, hearing, or ability to move. Making your content clear, making site navigation easy, and providing help for such people to see, read, or hear all support barrier-free accessibility. A clear design and a large enough font size—and/or the ability for the user to adjust font size—support readability for the visually impaired, as does an audio screen reader. You should be aware that people with impaired hearing will not be able to follow video and audio podcasts unless the content is also provided in subtitles. For elderly people or those with movement limitations, it is important that **links** can be easily clicked and forms can easily be filled out.

YOUR WEBSITE: BUSINESS CARD AND SHOP WINDOW

The COVID-19 lockdowns clearly showed the importance of a website for businesses. During that period, the website was often the only meeting point for businesses and their prospects and customers. A website is valuable—indeed, essential—and it should be well-thought-out and professional. Below are some important things to consider when you build or rebuild your website.

GOALS

Before you actually start building your website, you should be clear about the goals you want to achieve. Is it:

- raising awareness?
- increasing sales?
- increasing customer satisfaction?
- supporting your customer service?
- finding new prospects?
- burnishing your company's image?

You need to think about what your most important goals are because knowing this is essential to deciding how your website should be designed and what content should be included.

DESIGN

The design of your website has to be congruent with your brand and style guide (please refer to chapter 1). The focus should be on usability, enabling your visitors to quickly understand how to find the information they are looking for. Menu items and **links** should be easily recognizable. Put the most important information at the top of the site to allow users to see it without scrolling. Form and function have to clearly support the user's ability to find what they need to find on your site.

INFORMATION AND STRUCTURE

Be aware that a visitor may not know anything about your company, so try to walk in their shoes and explain in a clear manner how your offerings will benefit them. Nobody wants to read page-long essays, so make these explanations short and easy to understand. Use bullet points! It should be a no-brainer that the content on your website has to be good and authentic to satisfy your visitors, but it is also necessary to meet search engine requirements. Your website should have a clear structure, with the following elements:

- **Home page**
- Products and services
- Blog and/or news
- Case studies, testimonials, and reviews
- FAQs
- About us
- Getting in touch
- Legal notices

Let's talk a little more about each of these.

HOME PAGE

The first page should explain what you are doing and why someone should buy from you and not your competitors (your USP, unique selling proposition; please refer to chapter 3). It should deliver any important news or special offers, and it should make the rest of your site easily accessible via a clear website structure with cross-links to the **subpages**. Including a search bar for users is certainly the best way for your website visitors to quickly find exactly the information they are looking for. This is an important feature for your website, so be sure to ask for it when hiring an individual or agency to work on your website.

PRODUCTS AND SERVICES

In order to convince your website visitors to get in touch, to motivate them to want to learn more about your products and services, you should have clear, consistent, and engaging descriptions of what you offer. Videos and pictures can help a lot in this regard (but please mind loading times!). Special offers can work as lead generators, providing additional motivation for site visitors to get in touch with you.

BLOG AND/OR NEWS

A blog is a perfect tool to highlight your expertise and to bind prospects or customers to your company. It might also be important to **link** to reports or research relevant to your business. This is where people will find the most opportunities to utilize **links** and have other people in their industry share their posts. If your company gets mentioned in magazines or newspapers, this is also the place to **link** to those articles. Please also refer to chapter 7 for my advice on writing a blog.

CASE STUDIES, TESTIMONIALS, AND REVIEWS

Provided your customers agree to be featured or have their information shared, you can describe projects that you have already completed and/or products you have sold. This can be a great way to authenticate and emphasize your expertise. Ask satisfied customers to describe how happy they are with your products and services and maybe even provide pictures or videos. This inspires confidence in prospects, helping them overcome possible barriers that might prevent them from getting in touch with you.

FAQS

Having a page with frequently asked questions (FAQs) enables your prospects to get answers about your products and services without having to get in touch with you. This saves time for them and you, and it can help to overcome doubts regarding what you offer. Knowing your customers and your business as you do, it should be easy for you to put together a list of questions you have often heard about your business and answer them in a clear and helpful way.

ABOUT US

The About Us page is, naturally, about your company and, if you desire, your team. These pages can help generate trust and convince prospects that you are the company to work with because they can demonstrate your training, experience, and expertise.

GETTING IN TOUCH

It is also very important to provide an uncomplicated way for prospects to contact you. The telephone number especially should be placed in a very prominent position and be clickable with a smartphone. You would not believe how many unclickable phone numbers are still out there on websites, totally ignoring the kind of convenience that phone users have come to expect. Including your address and high-lighting your location on a map is especially important when you are a brick-and-mortar store customers tend to visit in person, such as a local business serving your neighborhood. Business hours have to be reliable and easily found. If you decide to use a contact form that can be filled out on your website, be sure to follow all of the privacy laws regarding processing the data you get via this method—and be sure to actually respond quickly whenever someone gets in touch with you.

LEGAL NOTICES

Your website must have the following:

- A legal disclosure showing your company name with contact data such as phone number, email, registered address, and registered company number

- Data protection statement explaining which data are stored, how long they are used, and how they are shared, and including information of the user's data protection rights (access, correction, deletion, complaint, withdrawal of consent)

- Page with your terms and conditions

- **Cookie**-law-compliant consent to **cookies** request for all websites that are owned within the EU or are aimed at customers in the EU—including an explanation of how the **cookie** information will be used; a mechanism for getting consent from visitors for your storing or retrieving any information on their computer, smartphone or tablet; and an explanation of how their consent can be withdrawn

MY SPECIAL ADVICE

Meeting legal requirements is a condition to being online. Making mistakes in this area can cause legal trouble and engender fines—sometimes sizable ones. To avoid this, I recommend asking your legal advisor to go through your legal disclosure, **cookie** information, and data protection statement, as well as your terms and conditions. If you have chosen the "Do It for Me" or "Do It with Me" approach to develop your website, your provider or partner should know the legal framework and should guarantee that your online presence will comply with current legal requirements.

BUILDING PROFESSIONAL LANDING PAGES

Landing pages are located either within your website to highlight special offers or are launched separately to promote a special product or service. Users can be guided to your landing pages from online ads, search results, email notices, social media postings, blog posts, or any other effective launch points. Landing pages need to contain exactly the information and/or offer users are looking for and should include a strong **call to action (CTA).** They should focus on the one topic they are specifically designed for and include no distractions from that topic. This is the main difference between landing pages and websites. Websites offer many possibilities for exploration and many sources of information, allowing users to gain as much information about a company as possible. Landing pages focus on one topic.

Users will go to a landing page to:

- Get further information about a product/service

- Register for a special service

- Get an offer for a product/service

- Purchase a product/service

ELEMENTS OF A SUCCESSFUL LANDING PAGE

Here are some tips for putting together an effective landing page:

- Whether the landing page is part of your website or separate from it, it should be designed in the same distinctive way as your website to ensure that users are aware it belongs to your company.

- It should reference the source the user is coming from. For example, if you're a garden appliance store that wants to promote the latest lawnmower, the landing page has to show the details of that specific lawnmower, not a broad introduction to garden appliances. If the prospect comes, for example, from an ad, the landing page should have the same design as the ad and refer to the ad's content.

HEADLINES AND SUBHEADLINES[8]

- Headlines should clearly state what the landing page is all about—they have to be as specific as possible.

---

8   For additional information, check out: Luke Heinecke, "11 Ways To Write Wildly Profit-able Landing Page Headlines," Linear.com, January 15, 2020, accessed September 2021, https://lineardesign.com/blog/landing-page-headlines/.

- Subheadlines should correspond with the headline, clarifying the headline and further explaining what the user can expect.

- Numbers in headlines increase click rates and conversions—for example, "Ten Ways to Prepare Your Garden for Spring."

- Five to nine words is the optimum length for headlines and subheadlines.

- Negative headlines actually show better results than positive ones. For example, "Not Getting Your Chimney Cleaned Could Lead to Fire!"

ELEMENTS OF CLEAR AND EASY-TO-UNDERSTAND CONTENT[9]

- Be clear of the purpose of your landing page.

- Be aware of similar landing pages published by your competitors.

- Be aware of your audience and the reason why they are visiting your landing page.

- Write in clear language your audience will understand and enjoy reading.

- Use bullet points and structure your text for better understanding.

---

9 For additional information, check out: "Landing Page Best Practices," Unbounce. com, https://unbounce.com/landing-page-articles/landing-page-best-practices/; and Sharon Hurley Hall, "8 Tips On How to Write a Great Landing Page Content: Examples & Strategies," TaboolaBlog.com, May 28, 2020, accessed September 2021, https://blog.taboola.com/how-to-write-landing-page-content/.

- Use facts and figures and, if possible, testimonials to provide proof for what you're saying.

- Put your **call to action** in a very prominent spot—for example, register for a service, download of a white paper—where it can't be missed.

- Phone numbers and contact details should be placed prominently as well.

- Be aware that a landing page does not necessarily need to follow a logical top-to-bottom structure; it may be better to start with the most convincing argument or the **call to action** to catch the reader's attention.

- Use responsive design, just as you should on your website, so the landing page is optimized for whatever device the user employs.

- Don't forget the legal information, which is required on a landing page as well as on a website.

USING A CONTENT MANAGEMENT SYSTEM

A **content management system** (CMS) helps you keep your website up to date and fresh. Even if the website was designed by an agency in a DIFM or DIWM mode, having a **CMS** will enable you to make corrections or updates to the website on your own. This way, you can save money and time because you won't need help from the website's designer—provided, of course, that the change is not something that has to be done by a technical or design expert. When you plan your website with an agency, make sure it's built in such a way that you can make these changes on your own.

With a **CMS**, you are able to do the following:

- Work on your website's content—write new text, change data such as operating hours, and add blogs and pictures and videos.

- Save the new content.

- Show the content correctly on your website.

When selecting a **CMS**, it should ideally have the following features:

- Is easy to understand without your having to study a user manual.

- Allows you to integrate additional functions such as a calendar, an order system, and a web shop.

- Works on mobile devices.

- Allows teams to collaboratively plan, schedule, and execute content strategies.

- Is protected from hacks and malware. (Note that open-source **CMSs** are not fully protected against hackers.)

- Provides access for multiple users.

The big advantage of a **CMS** is your ability to constantly add up-to-date content on your website, such as revising hours during holiday seasons, adding new products, and putting up new sales offers. Since search engines favor fresh, up-to-date content, your website will have a higher **SEO** ranking.

WordPress is one of the free-of-charge open-source systems, but I strongly recommend Wix.com. This is a great tool for the majority of websites. It is easy to use and offers a huge variety of add-ons.

TEST, TEST, TEST WEBSITES AND LANDING PAGES

Some of the ways you should test your website and landing pages before going live with them are as follows:

- Do **A/B tests** to show which content, structure, illustrations, etc., will work out best for your users. Such tests are the only reliable way to know which websites and landing pages will be most effective.

- Test the load times to ensure that users will not be so frustrated that they'll leave.

- Test your website and landing pages on different devices to be sure that they look and function well on each of them.

INCREASING WEBSITE TRAFFIC

After putting much effort into building your website, you, of course, want to have as many visitors as possible. Putting significant effort into high-quality **SEO** is essential for bringing visitors to your page—and not just any visitors, but those who have already looked for the products and services you are selling on a search engine. Such users have already shown a high interest in your offerings and are therefore highly valuable. Above, we already have discussed all the aspects of **SEO** you should be aware of when building your website.

Besides your efforts at **SEO**, you should take advantage of every opportunity to publish your web address—in your emails, letters, and invoices, of course, but also on your company car(s), which is a free-of-charge channel for advertising your web presence.

Additionally, you should take care that you are findable always and anywhere your clients or prospects might look for your products and services. In the next chapter, you'll learn more about this.

KEY TAKEAWAYS

- Before developing a website, take your time to consider well how much time and effort you are able to commit to building the site. These considerations will help to decide which model is best for you: DIY, DIFM, or DIWM.

- No matter how much effort you yourself put into building your website, be sure to aim for the highest possible quality website building tool or website provider/publisher. Always keep in mind that the website is your business card and your shop window.

- In order to be listed and seen on search engines, your website has to meet special quality requirements, starting with good and up-to-date content, use of responsive design, and a fast loading time. These qualities are great for the users of your website and for search engines, which favor any website qualities that increase user-friendliness.

- A **CMS** will help you continually add new material and keep your website fresh. You also need to test your website to make sure it functions well on all devices.

- Having a user on your website is a great opportunity to convince them that you are the appropriate business to work with. Therefore, consider carefully what a prospect or customer wants to know about your offering, and deliver this information in a clear, consistent, and easy-to-understand way.

- Check out the law, so you follow the rules for online presence, or ask your legal advisor to make sure your website meets all legal requirements.

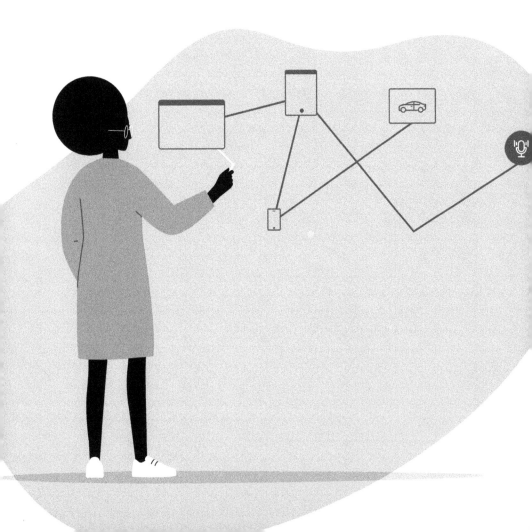

CHAPTER FIVE

HOW CAN MY CUSTOMERS FIND ME?

BEING PRESENT ANYTIME, ANYWHERE WITH ACTUAL DATA

■　　■　　■

B e found everywhere! There is no such thing as being *too* available! You need to be present where your prospects are searching for products and services like yours. Based on the media consumption data from your **buyer personas**, you might find them on search engines, social media, Pinterest, YouTube, etc. Wherever they find you, it's most important that they find authentic and correct information about your company in those places.

We have learned that it is critical for digital consumers to be able to view not just your information but your *correct* information. Far too often on the internet, consumers are confronted with false data and misinformation. To avoid this, you

> There is no such thing as being too available!

need to pay close attention to where your company is listed and whether or not your information is correct in every channel. Being present but with incorrect or false data will cause potential clients to doubt the seriousness and veracity of your company—and be assured that they will hold *your company* accountable for the false information, not *the portal* where you are listed.

Incorrect data not only causes a lack of confidence in your company but can also lead to serious real-world problems. For example, if the wrong hours of business for your company appear on a portal guiding a potential customer to your office or store, that person can end up standing in front of a locked door—which means you've probably lost a prospect to your competitor forever.

The more often you can be found, the more attention and clicks you will get. Adapt your content for related channels and/or use the same content on several channels—always keeping in mind your customer profiles and **buyer personas.**

Here are a few more rules about having a successful presence on the internet:

- Be found everywhere and anytime! Google, Bing, Facebook—there really is no such thing as being too available. The international consulting firm KPMG says that the number one reason consumers shop online is that they can do it at any time of the day—so your website needs to be available twenty-four hours a day.[10]

- Make sure your information is correct—everywhere! Getting information to consumers is useless if that information is inaccurate.

---

10   "The truth about online consumers," KPMG International Cooperative, 2017, accessed September 2021, https://assets.kpmg/content/dam/kpmg/xx/pdf/2017/01/the-truth-about-online-consumers.pdf.

IMPORTANCE OF SEARCH ENGINE MARKETING

Many, many consumers start their purchase journeys online. A survey by Statista in March 2020 showed that nearly half of online shoppers worldwide use search engines this way.[11] Another survey shows the online sources preferred by consumers worldwide to search for products. During the February and March 2020 survey period, 63 percent of online shoppers went to Amazon to start searching for products![12] Among search engines, Google currently holds 92.41 percent of the world's total search engine market share—and in Europe, it is even higher: 93.2 percent.[13]

Studies show that the purchase journey starting on search engines[14]

- includes viewing content about a company before actually talking to a salesperson from the company;

- brings a higher close rate than outbound leads (cold calling, direct mail, etc.);

---

11   Tugba Sabanoglu, "Online sources for product searches worldwide 2020," Statista, December 1, 2020, accessed September 2021, https://www.statista.com/statistics/1034209/global-product-search-online-sources/#statisticContainer.

12   "Online sources used by consumers worldwide to start searching for products as of March 2020," Statista, accessed September 2021, https://www.statista.com/statistics/1034209/global-product-search-online-sources/#statisticContainer.

13   "Search Engine Market Share Worldwide," StatCounter.com, accessed March 2021, https://gs.statcounter.com/search-engine-market-share.

14   Pat Ahern, "27 Mind-Bottling SEO Stats for 2021," Intergrowth.co, April 9, 2021, accessed September 2021, https://inter-growth.co/seo-stats/.

- increases the probability that consumers who search for a business nearby visit a local shop and actually buy a product or service within twenty-four hours; and

- usually includes looking up the location of the business on Google Maps.

The reason sales are more likely with people who search online is that they already have a clear desire in mind, know what they need, and just have to find the best and most appropriate company to deliver the products and services they want. This is also true for consumers using the internet Yellow Pages. Neither search engines nor the Yellow Pages are used just for the fun of it, like an online magazine. They are used because there is a special need that the consumer wants satisfied. For this reason, you have to make sure that your business is easily found on search engines. In this chapter, you will learn how to make this happen.

SEARCH ENGINE OPTIMIZATION

Search engine optimization (SEO) is the best way to make sure your company appears prominently in search engine results—and besides, the costs for paying an agency or individual **SEO** expert to help you improve your **SEO** ranking avoids extra media spending. To take advantage of this opportunity, your website has to fulfill certain quality criteria, such as having authentic content, fast loading time, and a number of technical factors. Please refer back to chapter 4 to learn more about using **SEO** effectively to make your website appear in a favorable position in search results.

GOOGLE BUSINESS PROFILE

Google Business Profile (formerly Google My Business) is another free-of-charge tool that enables your company to be listed on Google. Therefore you should put some effort to be (correctly) listed there and to keep your most important data actual. To list your business:

Sign in to your Google account and create your company profile.

- Enter your business name.

- Enter the radius or the areas you are working in.

- Enter the segment you are working in.

In order to take full advantage of Google, you should add relevant data about your business, such as the following:

- Business hours

- Website URL

- Specifics about what your business offers

- Logo

- Photos of your shop, employees, and products

- Videos demonstrating what your company does

Google's API update in February 2021 now allows a business to specify unique hours of operation. For example, a restaurant is open from 11:30 a.m. to 10:00 p.m. but delivers takeaway food from 11:00 a.m. to 9:00 p.m. Depending on the primary category with Google, the types of unique hours include categories such as (but not limited to) the following:

- Delivery hours

- Takeaway hours

- Pickup hours

- Kitchen hours

- Drive-through hours

- Brunch hours

- Happy hours

After Google has verified your business, your business will show up across Google platforms, such as Maps and Search.

When you are listed on Google, consumers can publish reviews and ratings for your business, and you can comment on those reviews and ratings immediately because you will be alerted whenever there is a new entry. To optimize your listing, you can ask your happy customers to publish a review and/or upload a picture of your business or product. To take full advantage of Google, you have to make sure your company data is always authentic and up to date.

The possible benefits of a Google Business Profile are many, often including

- higher visibility;

- easier for consumers to reach you;

- more traffic generated for your website;

- more visits to your online or bricks-and-mortar store; and

- increased revenue.[15]

---

15   For further information, visit the Google Business Profile Help Center at https://support.google.com/business.

SOCIAL MEDIA

Due to their massive usage, social media platforms have to be taken into account for reaching your prospects and customers. The usage data speaks for itself (see chapter 8), so you should make sure you can be found via social media platforms. Since there are a large number of such platforms, you can't use them all, so you should carefully consider which social media channels you want to use to reach out to consumers. Although you have to select these channels carefully, it is advantageous to have your company data available on social media channels so prospects or customers can easily get in touch with you. There is so much misinformation on the internet, so you have to make sure your data is correct and prevent false entries about your company by third parties. Please refer to chapter 8 for more details about how to use social media.

> Due to their massive usage, social media platforms have to be taken into account for reaching your prospects and customers.

VOICE SEARCH

Introduced in 2011 by Google, voice search was a novelty. Now, voice search is available via Siri, Alexa, Google Assistant, Cortana, and other tools. It is regularly used by consumers—predominantly via mobile phones—to search for companies, products, directions, and other practical information. With the popularity of smart speakers in households, such as Google Home or Apple HomePod, voice technologies have drastically improved in order to keep pace with consumer demand.

According to the studies of DataReportal, 46.7 percent of internet users aged sixteen to sixty-four worldwide use voice interfaces each month. Of course, younger internet users are driving this trend, with well over 50 percent of internet users below the age of thirty-five saying that they have used voice interfaces in the past thirty days.[16]

In a blog of the US agency DBS Interactive, it is summarized: "Trends show voice search users are increasingly searching for local results. Within the past year, 58 percent of consumers have found local businesses using voice search. And not only is the number of voice search *users* on the rise, but the number of voice *searches* also continues to grow, as 46 percent of those users will repeatedly use voice search to find a local business on a daily basis."[17]

You can only expect digital assistants to know the correct information about your company if you put it out there and ensure that it's accurate. The foundation of any voice search strategy is to organize and centralize all publicly available information about your people, products, and locations. You need a single, reliable, consistent data source that you can easily maintain and update.

DBS Interactive furthermore points out:[18] "Since voice search is often used to conduct local searches, it's important for merchants to keep their Google My Business listing and eCommerce stores in proper order with up-to-date operating information." Again, it is highly important to make sure websites are optimized for search engines and mobile devices by making sure your content is optimized

---

16 Simon Kemp, "Digital 2021 April Global Statshot Report," DataReportal, April 21, 2021, accessed September 2021, https://datareportal.com/reports/digital-2021-april-global-statshot.

17 "Voice Search Statistics and Emerging Trends," DBS Interactive, accessed September 2021, https://www.dbswebsite.com/blog/trends-in-voice-search/. See also: "The Growing Popularity of Voice Search," Creativo, September 22, 2019, https://creativouae.com/the-growing-popularity-of-voice-search.

18 "Voice Search Statistics and Emerging Trends," DBS Interactive.

and current. DBS Interactive goes on to suggest you do this "by eliminating duplicate pages, outdated contact information, and old operating hours"[19] because "roughly 75 percent of voice search results will rank in the top three positions for a particular question on a desktop search."[20]

HELPFUL TOOLS

Considering all of the portals, sites, and search engines you need to take into account, it might seem impossible to oversee them all and make sure that your authentic, accurate data are published. But you can relax—because help is available. Companies such as Yext or Uberall provide an easy way for you to control and manage how your business appears online or in voice searches. When you are working with a professional agency, be sure they have a cooperative relationship with Yext, Uberall, or a similar provider. These companies help you to make sure your business listings appear correctly across the internet and can be found on Google, Amazon Alexa, Apple Maps, Facebook, Foursquare, Yelp, and other leading third-party apps, maps, and social networks. Your data is posted on one centralized platform and distributed on all of the apps, maps, social networks, and search engines that matter most to your customers. You can even add pictures, videos, and content to motivate users to get in touch with you. Also, if your company gets a rating or review on the related portals, you are immediately alerted, which enables you to reply to the rating or review quickly.

---

19   "Voice Search Statistics and Emerging Trends," DBS Interactive.

20   Nolan Rosen, "Top 10 SEO Optimization Trends for 2020," CMOSolution. com, accessed September 2021, https://www.cmosolution.com/articles/ search-engine-marketing/top-10-seo-optimization-trends-for-2020.

PAID TRAFFIC: SEARCH ENGINE ADVERTISING (SEA) AND ONLINE ADVERTISING

To get traffic to your website, you can invest advertising money to the extent you need or want it. When investing in advertising, your goals should be:

- Measuring results

- Reaching website traffic goals you cannot reach otherwise

- Getting the best return on investment (ROI)

SEARCH ENGINE ADVERTISING (SEA)

SEA is a form of paid advertisement that places your ad among the top search results a search engine produces. It is linked to certain **keywords**, and whenever a user enters those **keywords**, it appears on top or on the right side of the results page. It can be a text-based ad or a product-listing ad with pictures of a product and is marked as an advertisement.

SEA is a perfect add-on to your **SEO** activities. If **SEO** is done correctly and professionally, your website is listed among the top results of a search engine, as mentioned in chapter 4, but with **SEA**, you can make sure your offering is definitely shown prominently on the first result page, without taking into account how well your **SEO** is functioning.

MY SPECIAL ADVICE

Before buying an **SEA** campaign, you have to diligently consider the **keywords** your potential customers might enter into a search engine. When selecting your **keywords**, you should think about the **customer journey** and be as precise as possible. If your selection is too broad, you will get clicks that cost money but do not lead to the desired result. **Keyword** tools like ads.google.com, Ubersuggest, or AnswerThePublic can give you insight into which **keywords** are used and how often, which competitors are using these **keywords**, and even whether it is worthwhile to use the most common **keywords** or would be more cost effective to employ less used **keywords** that target the same user. It is often more efficient to use niche **keywords**.

You also have to think about the **keywords** you want to exclude because they indicate things that are not part of your offering. For example, if you were a hairdresser who is only for women, you would exclude "barbershop" because that would attract men.

Next, you have to decide how much you want to pay for a click. Additionally, you have to make sure your ad is highly relevant to the consumers you are trying to reach. The click budget and relevance of the ad decide the ad rank and the position where your ads are shown on the result page.

To make the most out of your investment, you also have to **link** to a proper landing page, as outlined in chapter 4, leading the user from your ad directly to the action you want to trigger—placing an order, asking for a cost estimate, setting up an appointment, etc.

These considerations show that **SEA** is a pretty complicated advertising form. It is highly recommended that you get professional help in order to achieve the best results at the lowest cost. Wrongly done, it really can be a waste of money.

ONLINE ADVERTISING

In addition to **search engine advertising**, placing online ads is still a common way to advertise products and services and to reinforce a brand. There are many different formats based on specific portals. The ads **link** directly to the advertiser's website or landing page. Their effectiveness can be well measured, and the ways portals charge for online advertising are diverse. The most common are:

- **Cost-per-Impression:** Cost for a visual contact or the page retrieval of an entire HTML document with a browser—page impressions are usually not assigned to a specific user.

- **Cost-per-Mille:** Cost per thousand impressions.

- **Cost-per-View:** Cost for every instance an ad or video is seen—the pricing is used in online marketing, social media marketing, and video marketing; in video marketing, metrics usually only count if the viewer engages with the video and clicks on the play or skip button.

- **Cost-per-Click:** Cost for a click on an ad; this is very common and is used on many portals.

- **Cost-per-Lead:** Cost for a special predefined action, such as a newsletter registration or a download.

- **Cost-per-Order** or **Cost-per-Sale:** Cost per order or purchase.

While search engine ads are usually text based, the opportunities to create online ads that are more than text are nearly endless, including banner ads, videos, and coupons. Each portal has its own formats and technical requirements. Nevertheless, there are international standards, such as those provided by the Interactive Advertising Bureau (IAB), regarding online advertising that most portals observe.

When designing an online ad campaign, be sure you think of your **buyer personas** (see chapter 2) and those buyers' pain points. Although this kind of advertisement allows you to be creative, you should deliver your message clearly and in a way that is easily understood. And don't forget to include a **call to action**. To reinforce your brand, be sure the images and wording are in line with your style guide.

For details on social media advertising, please refer to chapter 8!

REMARKETING

I am sure that you have had the experience of receiving a large number of similar offers after searching for a particular product. For example, after searching for a new refrigerator, you get offers for these appliances whenever you turn on your computer and surf the internet. This experience is caused by what is called **remarketing**—also known as **retargeting**. Visitors to websites are tracked using tracking methods such as **cookies** and tags in order to confront them with advertising that might be especially interesting to them for a certain predefined period.

The goal is to turn the users' attention to a website—very often the company website they had previously visited—to encourage them to finally buy the product seen before. This method is also used to address customers after a certain period to encourage them to buy again. For example, if you are selling garden appliances, you can target those customers who have bought a lawn mower in summer with ads presenting snow shovels in late autumn. But please be aware of the (strict) legal requirements about using **remarketing**.

MY SPECIAL ADVICE

When using **remarketing**, be sure you are excluding users from your target list who have already bought a product in your web shop. It is terribly annoying receiving ads for a product you have already bought—and it is a waste of money for the seller because the product has already been purchased. For example, very few people need another lawn mower soon after they've bought a new one! Additionally, you should limit the frequency with which your ads are displayed to your target group. Too often can be frustrating for the user and may even result in an aversion to your product.

AMAZON

As I've mentioned, consumers begin product searches on Amazon even more often than they do on a search engine. To reiterate, 63 percent of online shoppers go to Amazon to start searching for products (just to reemphasize the importance of search engines)! So obviously, if you are selling physical products, Amazon is a selling platform you should at least consider.

To sell on Amazon, you can choose between paying a fixed monthly fee, for which you can sell an unlimited number of products, or a fee per product sold. Additionally, you have to carefully decide which Amazon product categories are best for your products and how your products meet Amazon's requirements.

After doing all this preliminary work, you have to carefully define the price for your products. Due to Amazon's sales rankings based on sales figures, it is important not to be too expensive, so you can achieve the highest possible volume of sales. Free-of-charge services, such as free delivery, can also support your sales strategy.

With the Amazon Seller Center, you can keep track of your orders. Fulfillment by Amazon also enables you to deliver your products to your customers—if you are not willing to, or capable of, handling delivery on your own.

To have your products be visible among the thousands and thousands of products Amazon offers, you have to be sure they are well described to potential customers. Therefore, you should diligently include product name, brand, category, **keywords**, product description, pictures, and details regarding delivery and payment.

Since Amazon attaches great importance to the satisfaction of its customers, it is essential that you get many good reviews of your store on Amazon. But even more important than good reviews for your products is offering good products. If available, you should include **links** to blogs or other publications that refer favorably to your products. Finally, there are many advertising possibilities on Amazon that will help put your products in front of potential customers.

Although Amazon is a great way to quickly get your products in front of a huge audience, you need to be aware of the disadvantages, which range from high fees to facing thousands and thousands of competitors, which force you to sell your goods at the lowest possible price.[21]

Keeping this in mind, it certainly is worthwhile considering building your own web shop. Please refer to chapter 6 to learn more about web shops!

CASE STUDY:
BOEREN & BUREN

When you promote a special sales offer, the landing page customers go to should have a **call to action** that fits the media channel from which the consumer has come. DexVille found the perfect match of these elements to successfully market seasonal fruits and vegetables to the right target group.

THE COMPANY

Boeren & Buren is a short-chain network in Flanders and is part of an international organization founded in France in 2011. Through Boeren & Buren, consumers can buy delicious, fresh seasonal products at fair prices directly from farmers and artisan producers. The online platform built for this short supply chain brings consumers and producers closer together, helping the farmers and artisan producers to sell their products and consumers to find them conveniently.

---

21   For more information about selling on Amazon, visit "Become an Amazon Seller" at https://sell.amazon.com.

THE CHALLENGE

DexVille started by building a brand awareness strategy to promote the concept of the Boeren & Buren online platform using social and Google search channels. The goal was to reach a new audience in Flanders with interest in vegetables, fruits, and other fresh foods. In May, Boeren & Buren wanted to launch a campaign around "The Week of the Short Chain" with a specific activation to generate more sales.

THE SOLUTION

DexVille created a dedicated landing page with searchable content about the short supply chain and the other advantages of using the Boeren & Buren platform. Spring was the perfect time for a new audience to discover the easy availability of fresh products in the region and to try these products. The **call to action** was to order locally during "The Week of the Short Chain" using a discount promotional code.

THE RESULT

The campaign raised regional awareness by being broadcast on Facebook and Google Display, and this awareness generated an excellent conversion rate among those who were targeted.

KEY TAKEAWAYS

- Make sure you have carefully defined the data of your company (contact data, operating hours, etc.) and that this information is consistent on all media platforms.

- To optimize your digital presence, consider using a professional tool that will ensure your company is found online anytime and anywhere, with correct data.

- Since search engines are the top entry portals for your potential customers searching for a product, you need to be accessible on them.

- For search engines, you have to use all free-of-charge possibilities to be listed there, such as **search engine optimization (SEO)** of your website and listing yourself on Google. Additionally, you can consider purchasing paid search engine advertisements.

- In case you decide to be present on Amazon, be careful to list your products in a way that a potential customer will get the best possible insight into your offering. Also, paid ads might be necessary to put your offering on Amazon in front of the right consumers and enough consumers.

- After carefully considering the media consumption of your target audience, you might also want to purchase online advertising campaigns on certain portals appropriate for reaching that target audience.

- Good planning and monitoring—defining the goals and KPIs you want to reach as well as constantly checking the results of your activities—will help you to find the most cost-effective way to market your products and services.

CHAPTER SIX

HOW CAN MY CUSTOMERS BUY MY STUFF?

OPENING YOUR BUSINESS ONLINE

■ ■ ■

n 2020, over two billion people purchased goods or services online, and e-commerce sales surpassed US $4.2 trillion worldwide.[22]

A survey by DataReportal in the third quarter (Q3) of 2020 showed that, at a global level, nearly 77 percent of internet users aged sixteen to sixty-four had bought something online via some kind of device in the previous month. Despite these already high numbers, there was actually an *increase* of 3.3 percent in online purchasing between Q2 and Q3 2020, representing quarterly growth of more than 4.5 percent—probably due to the pandemic.[23]

---

22   Daniela Coppola, "E-commerce worldwide: Statistics & Facts," Statista, April 15, 2021, accessed September 2021, https://www.statista.com/topics/871/online-shopping/#dossierSummary.

23   Simon Kemp, "Digital 2021: Global Overview Report," DataReportal, January 27, 2021, accessed September 2021, https://datareportal.com/reports/digital-2021-global-overview-report.

E-commerce adoption in Europe matched the global trend: 85.5 percent of internet users in the UK aged sixteen to sixty-four bought something online via some device in the month before the survey. About 81 percent did so in Germany and Austria. In Belgium, 74.8 percent made a purchase online. In the Netherlands, it was 76.2 percent, and in France, 74.4 percent. Although there are not many differences in the level of online shopping enthusiasm due to age and gender, research clearly shows that younger people tend to use their mobile phones for shopping, while baby boomers usually stick to laptops or desktop computers to make online purchases.[24]

According to the report, many product and service categories profited from the rise of e-commerce. For example, there was a 41 percent increase in food and personal care purchases—the highest growth during the period when consumers had to stay at home during lockdowns or were avoiding going to supermarkets because of possible health risks. And it will not come as a surprise that online travel bookings suffered the most, with a 51 percent decrease in profit.[25]

> There are strong indications that these new online shopping patterns will remain prevalent, even after the COVID-19 danger has passed.

Finally, the report concludes that there are strong indications that these new online shopping patterns will remain prevalent, even after the COVID-19 danger has passed. Many consumers will likely continue to conduct a greater share of their shopping activities online. Additionally, significant parts of the buyer

---

24   Simon Kemp, "Digital 2021 April Global Statshot Report."

25   Simon Kemp, "Digital 2021 April Global Statshot Report."

journey, such as searching for information or comparing prices, will remain online permanently.[26]

NEGLECT OF E-COMMERCE IS A VERY BAD BUSINESS STRATEGY

COVID-19 has changed and will continue to change the world, and store owners are no longer able to avoid offering an online shop—even though many of them think they will.

This was borne out in Belgium during the coronavirus lockdowns. According to the *Gazet Van Antwerpen*, local retailers in the city turned to hastily established web shops to keep themselves above water—and they were successful. Local online orders increased 70 percent, and they were able to achieve 20 percent turnover.[27] The sad part of this story is that most retailers didn't put much effort into establishing high-quality web shops that would help sustain their businesses after the coronavirus pandemic passes.

"Unfortunately, our research shows that many retailers do not take their newly opened webshop seriously," said researcher Joris Beckers. "For example, only 25 percent of the retailers used a professional company … to set it up." And despite the general expectation that the coronavirus experience will change shopping habits permanently, 70 percent of shop owners surveyed "do not see the online store as an important sales channel in the future."[28] So these shop owners are apparently willing to cede revenue that could have

---

26   Simon Kemp, "Digital 2021 April Global Statshot Report."

27   "Majority of local merchants see online store as something temporary: 'Belgian money threatens to flow abroad,'" GVA, November 12, 2020, accessed September 2021, https://www.gva.be/cnt/dmf20201112_93915320.

28   "Majority of local merchants see online store as something temporary: 'Belgian money threatens to flow abroad.'"

been theirs to larger, more established online shopping sites such as Amazon.

The same reluctance to invest in online shops is shown by a 2020 analysis of the websites of SMBs in twelve European countries conducted by Siinda, the European Search & Information Industry Association, and Insites (former Silktide), a web intelligence company. According to this study, only 13 percent of SMB sites have an identifiable e-commerce solution. Unfortunately, neglecting to build a professional e-commerce strategy will turn out to be very damaging for these businesses. Even without COVID-19 in the picture, the movement toward e-commerce cannot be turned back.[29]

RESEARCH ONLINE, PURCHASE OFFLINE (ROPO)

Consumers not only buy online but also go online to get information about the products and services they intend to buy, checking out prices, ratings, and availability. Very often, they do this before going to a shop to buy in person the goods or services they have selected online. And due to increasing mobile usage, customers often do their online research right in the store! This habit is called **ROPO (research online, buy offline)** and shows the tight connection between online and offline shopping. This process can also happen the other way around, when shoppers first go to stores to talk with informed salespeople and check out the goods they intend to buy and then order those products online, where they can usually find them for the cheapest price.

Another trend also pushes store owners to engage in e-commerce, and that is when products are selected and bought online but picked

---

29   "Landscape Survey," Siinda in cooperation with Insites (formerly Silktide), accessed August 2021, https://www.siinda.org/siinda-market-research.

up in person at the store (click and collect). This was especially popular during COVID-19 lockdowns when the shops were actually closed, but purchased goods were put in front of the shops, where consumers could pick them up without waiting or paying for a delivery service to bring them to their home. Another variation is "click and meet." In this situation, consumers could browse online and check out the offerings of a store. Then, when a product met their needs, they could make an appointment in the store to see the product close up and talk to a salesperson about it. This allows the store owner to plan the right number of sales personnel to have on hand and also meet the specifications regarding the number of customers per square meter established by their government during the pandemic.

If awareness of shopping patterns such as these is not enough to convince you to have a professionally done online shop, also consider the advantages of being able to present your full range of goods and services to potential customers on an electronic device, allowing you to shrink the sales area in your shop and reduce your rental costs.

Like it or not, physical and digital retail grow into each other—a development that some observers are referring to as "phygital retail," the blurring of the lines between physical retail and digital retail.[30]

GETTING STARTED WITH E-COMMERCE

Taking into account all of the considerations I've described, it should be clear there is really no way around opening an online store. The next question is: How do you go about setting it up? Basically, there are three approaches you can take:

---

30   Nicholas Moore, "What is Phygital Retail? Physical and digital retail, together," Storefront, November 23, 2020, accessed September 2021, https://www.thestorefront.com/mag/what-is-phygital-retail-physical-and-digital-retail-together.

- Do It Yourself (DIY)

- Do It for Me or Do It with Me (DIFM; DIWM)

- Use an established third-party marketplace

Let's examine each of these options.

> Taking into account all of the considerations I've described, it should be clear there is really no way around opening an online store.

DO IT YOURSELF (DIY)

If you choose the DIY solution when building a website, you have to take care of your own webspace and your domain. There are a large number of providers to choose from that can enable you to build your shop—from the free-of-charge WordPress to offerings such as WIX, which I can truly recommend. Although building your web shop is similar to building your website, you have to pay attention to certain topics, especially important for web shops.

When choosing a provider to use for this approach, make sure you can answer "yes" to the following questions about what the provider offers:

- Are there enough attractive templates to choose from for presenting your products?

- Will it be easy to upload descriptions and pictures of your products?

- Are the tools optimized for search engines, so people can find your products?

- Can you integrate a blog with text, pictures, and videos about your products?

- Is it possible to integrate all necessary legal requirements—for example, can the site be set up so that the terms and conditions and cancellation policy can be actively confirmed by the user?

- Is it possible to easily add additional products or services when you want to expand your web shop?

- Can you easily get support in case of questions or problems with the platform? Downtime for your shop costs you money directly!

- Is it possible to integrate text translation in order to serve a multilingual community?

DO IT FOR ME AND DO IT WITH ME (DIFM AND DIWM)

Probably the easiest and most time-saving approach for building your online shop is to hire a professional agency. The money you spend on an agency is usually well invested, and using professionals to do this for you allows you to concentrate on your offerings, branding, and other tasks. When you select an agency, you should define right at the beginning to what extent you can participate in building the shop, how changes can be made to the website after it is built, how new products can be integrated, and how additional website segments can be added—preferably by you, to allow flexibility and save money.

USE AN ESTABLISHED THIRD-PARTY MARKETPLACE

To save you the time, money, and effort of building your own shop, you can include your products on an existing shopping platform, such as Amazon (see chapter 5), eBay, Etsy, or another. The advantages are obvious, and the result is that you get a web shop without having to build and maintain it. You can immediately start selling products and benefit from the shop's existing brand awareness. On the other hand, the products offered there will not be linked to your company as directly and therefore will not support your brand as well. You also have to pay fees and are often forced to sell at the lowest possible price because of fierce competition in these marketplaces.

INGREDIENTS FOR A SUCCESSFUL ONLINE SHOP

There are some basics that you should keep in mind when opening an online shop:

- You should have a clear concept about what you want to sell, to whom, and at what price.

- Your shop has to be easily findable on the internet.

- You should make sure your products are listed and presented in a clear and easy-to-find way within your shop to enable your users to locate what they need, and you have to have a trustworthy shop that delivers on its promises.

- The customer's process, from finding the right product to payment to getting delivery, must be logical, easy to understand, and flawless in its execution.

- All legal requirements must be carefully observed.

- The after-sale contact with your customer, including confirmation of the order and delivery, should be courteous and helpful.

- You should be polite and generous about exchanges or returns.

- You should ask for ratings and reviews because prospects look for them.

- You need to find ways to cross-sell, making shoppers aware of other products and services you have that relate to what they're already buying.

A CLEAR CONCEPT

As always, a well-thought-out plan is the first step to success. Opening an online shop starts with considering who your customers are, defining profiles and personas (see chapter 2). And of course, you have to have a clear concept regarding your products and services. In chapter 3, I described how to define your unique selling proposition (USP). These basic considerations will help you to define how your online shop should look, what to offer there, and what your pricing should be.

To establish an online shop, you also need to figure out these considerations at the very beginning:

- Where your physical products will be stored

- How you'll handle buyer payments

- How products will be delivered

- How you'll organize the process from order to delivery

- How you'll handle returns and exchanges

GETTING CUSTOMERS

I cover customer acquisition in both chapters 4 and 5. In chapter 4, I talk about setting up a website with a special focus on **search engine optimization (SEO)**. In chapter 5, I talk about **search engine advertisement (SEA)** and other ways to make your website easy to find. Since an online shop is a website, everything explained there is, of course, also valid for your web shop.

YOUR VIRTUAL SHOP

When building your online shop, keep in mind that this virtual shop should meet many of the same requirements that a physical shop does. Your customers should feel comfortable entering your shop. They should be able to easily find what they are looking for. They should be able to get answers if they have questions about your products and services. They should be able to get recommendations from other customers, just as they'd ask friends and family about a physical shop.

For an online shop, it is crucial to do the following:

- Highlight the value and benefits of the products

- Make it clear who should buy the product and why

- Show physical products from every possible angle

- Offer zoom, so the user can get a very detailed picture of each physical product

- Integrate a video of the products in use

- Clearly display the prices of products

- Integrate bonus and sales offers

- Offer free trials or samples

- Provide reviews and ratings of the products

- Offer a delivery service (at additional cost if you wish)

- Put your **call to action** in a very prominent spot where it can't be missed.

Regarding product presentation, please also refer to the chapter 4 discussion of websites and landing pages.

As in a physical shop, it is important that you are available for your customers in case they have questions. Therefore, it should be easy for the user to find an FAQ section. Additionally, it should be easy to get in touch with you by phone and email. Very innovative companies might also think about integrating a chatbot to react to customer questions.

FLAWLESS PROCESS FROM ORDER TO PAYMENT

As soon as a customer selects a product, there should be an easily accessible button to add the product to a cart. The customer should constantly have the opportunity to check the contents of the cart and have the choice either to go to checkout or to continue shopping. It would also be wise to show additional products, which are somehow linked to the product already selected, at this stage of the purchase process. For example, if you are selling cosmetic products, you could show a night cream when the user has selected a day cream. When all products are selected, the purchase has to be completed simply, with a click on a purchase button.

The next step is getting the buyer's contact data. When asking for the user's data, including contact information, beware of asking for too much information, especially information you don't really need, because asking for too much increases the danger of losing a prospect. Also keep in mind that there can be different addresses for sending the invoice and for the delivery. If delivery is not free, the cost needs to be determined via postal code or address and clearly posted. If possible, offer delivery services at different speeds and costs. If you have a physical store, as well as a virtual one, you should make it possible for the purchase to be picked up at the store (note that this brings the customer into your physical store, where they might make additional purchases). If it's appropriate, and you want to do it, you can offer to deliver the products in gift wrapping.

It is important to get the customer's email address for further correspondence—to send a confirmation of the order, to inform them about when the goods are leaving the warehouse, to let them know when the purchase is being delivered, etc. When collecting the email address is also the right time to ask the customer for approval to send a newsletter (preferably emphasizing that the newsletter will include exclusive offers and discounts).

You should also offer different payment methods for the customer's convenience. PayPal is the preferred payment method among shoppers worldwide, and there are other payment services as well. The traditional credit card is the second preference, followed by debit cards.[31]

---

31   Daniela Coppola, "Global number of digital buyers 2014-2021," Statista, November 27, 2020, accessed September 2021, https://www.statista.com/statistics/251666/number-of-digital-buyers-worldwide/.

You may also include the opportunity to pay when the product is delivered.

The security program you choose for you and your customer should be your highest priority in order to make sure that the customer payments reach you. You can underline the security of your shop by applying for a special quality seal that is well known in your region, such as Trusted Shops, EMOTA (European Trustmark), and Secured Shop. This will convince your prospects that they can order goods at your store without being afraid of it being a bogus offering and losing their money.

After the purchase is done and the product is delivered, this is the perfect opportunity to ask the customer to write a review because their attention is still focused on the product. Of course, you also have to be prepared that your customer will not like a product. In this case, you have to make sure it can be easily sent back. Although it is always disappointing to have a purchase canceled, you should be generous in how you handle returns because this will enable you to retain the relationship with your customer and make it more likely that they'll want to buy from you again.

LEGAL REQUIREMENTS

To avoid any legal problems, be sure your shop meets all of the legal requirements covered in chapter 4 for websites as well as those especially important for web shops: the legal disclosure; terms and conditions to be clicked on before the purchase is completed; privacy policy, including the use of **cookies**; the right of withdrawal; the right of return and exchange; etc. I highly recommend asking your legal advisor to ensure that your web shop meets all legal requirements.

AFTER THE SALE

After the purchase is done and the goods are delivered, you can start the after-sale process—provided that your customer has given you permission to send emails or use **cookies**. Based on the product bought, you can offer similar products in due course and integrate this customer into your cross-selling activities. This can be done via newsletters or by **retargeting**. In the case of **retargeting**, be sure to exclude the product that was already bought. **Retargeting** might also be a perfect tool when a product was put into a customer's cart but not purchased. Delivering online ads about this product and perhaps even a discount offer could be the final push needed to convince the user to finally make the purchase. You might also send free trials of a new product to a shopper who bought similar goods online and ask them to write a review for the new product.

If a customer is happy with your product and with the ordering, purchasing, and delivery processes, it is very likely he or she will buy again in your shop. It is certainly easier for consumers to rely on a shop that has already proved to be good and reliable than it is to try out a new, unknown shop. You can also strengthen the customer relationship by implementing a loyalty program, with which the more products someone buys in your shop, the higher the discount you give them, or something along those lines. Please refer to chapter 2 about cross-selling and chapter 5 about **retargeting**. In this next chapter, we'll talk about the details of email marketing.

KEY TAKEAWAYS

- Studies show there is no way *not* to do e-commerce.

- Shopping habits like **ROPO (research online, purchase offline)** show that web shops are important even if you have a successful physical shop.

- When setting up an online shop, consider the pros and cons of different possibilities, from DIY to using a shopping platform.

- When building your online shop, provide the same amenities as in your physical shop—such as making sure products can be found easily and providing helpful customer service.

- Take the utmost care in the process from ordering to delivery and return/exchange.

- Be aware of the very strict legal requirements of e-commerce.

- Take full advantage of the after-sales opportunities.

CHAPTER SEVEN

HOW DO I TALK TO MY CUSTOMERS?

TAKING ADVANTAGE OF CAREFULLY SELECTED CHANNELS

■　　■　　■

S mall business owners can no longer rely only on word-of-mouth publicity to promote their businesses. They need a robust strategy that takes advantage of all the ways they communicate with customers and potential customers. From webpages and social media to online stores and Google search results, small business owners have a plethora of channels through which to communicate with consumers—and consumers expect to be able to learn about companies through a reasonable number of these channels. What you are selling is what should dictate how you try to sell it, but the most important thing to keep in mind is: keep selling! If you rest on your laurels, your business can atrophy quickly, because today your customers and potential customers have many choices about where to get virtually any kind of product or service.

If you want to attract customers, you need to understand why and how people are buying, or want to buy, what you are selling (chapter 2)—and then you need to align your channel strategy with where they are and where they want you to be. Once you collect data about your customers and build customer profiles, you will have a clear picture of their buying habits and what kind of communications they are willing to receive. And your communication via these channels should be clear, consistent, and frequent in order to define the benefits of your products and services, raise interest in them, answer questions and counter objections about them, and hopefully motivate existing customers to spread the news about your offerings to colleagues and/or friends and family.

> Small business owners can no longer rely only on word-of-mouth publicity to promote their businesses.

Communication with your customers has to be tailor-made for them using the sociodemographic information I talked about collecting in chapter 2 to get a picture of your **buyer personas** (age, gender, income, buying habits, etc.). This is essential for defining a successful way to talk to your customers. For example, customers who respond emotionally have to be addressed in a way that rouses their emotions, while customers who make fact-based decisions need all the data up front. To demonstrate what this means, let's consider what you would do if your business was selling cosmetic products and treatments to women.

For the emotional approach, you could describe the feelings that using your products and enjoying your treatments will arouse in customers, such as attractiveness, feeling younger and more beautiful. You could say something such as, "Your colleagues, family, and friends will be amazed at how great you look!"

For a facts-oriented customer, you could emphasize the healthy ingredients of the products—how they are produced, what effects they will have on the body, how the biology works—even referring to medical studies, if available. You could use a pitch such as, "Our products and treatments have been proven to promote healthier skin."

After developing clear insight into who your buyers are and how to address them, you need to be aware of where each of them is on the **customer journey**. You need to understand the different stages of relationships that customers have with your company—from the customer's point of view. You need to analyze the different touch points along the way, from their first contact with your offerings to their becoming a faithful customer willing to spread the news regarding your great service.[32]

In order to do this, you should be able to answer these questions about your customers:

- How does a potential customer become aware of your company: Advertising? Social media? Recommendations by friends? Searching online?

- How can you turn that awareness into real interest, a willingness to engage with your company?

- How can this interest in and engagement with your company lead to a purchase?

- What is each of the touch points that occur when someone does business with you—from inquiry to order entry to billing to getting them to review your products and services?

- How can you get a customer to buy a product and service again—or, even better, to buy additional products and services?

---

32   For more information on understanding a customer journey, check out Jay Baer's article "How to Create a Personalized Digital Customer Journey" on Emarsys.com at https://emarsys.com/learn/blog/creating-personalized-experience-across-digital-customer-journey/, accessed September 2021.

- How can you get new customers via recommendations by the customer, turn the customer into a brand advocate/promoter?

The different stages of the **customer journey** can be described using the AIDA funnel:[33]

- Awareness > Market potential

- Interest > Suspects

- Desire > Prospects

- Action > Customers

This is an old traditional marketing approach but still has its merits to understand a **customer journey** from the first contact to purchase. However, the internet and social media have added complexity to the stages of creating initial awareness of your products and services, turning interested consumers into customers, and turning customers into brand advocates.

Once you understand what your customers want from you and where they are on the **customer journey**, you can start to define your channels and channel strategies for reaching those customers for various reasons:

- Getting new leads and customers

- Turning leads into buying customers

- Motivating existing customers to buy again and buy other things

- Asking customers to be brand promoters

I will discuss each of these channels and their strategies below.

---

33   "AIDA Formula," Unternehmer.de, accessed August 2021, https://unternehmer.de/lexikon/online-marketing-lexikon/aida-formel.

GETTING NEW LEADS AND CUSTOMERS

Based on your **customer personas** (please refer to chapter 2!), you can figure out what kind of media to use to address potential customers. Is it the local newspaper, the billboard in the local soccer stadium, your booth at a trade fair, Instagram and YouTube? Keep in mind that the majority of searches for products and services start online now, so you *must* make sure that your company can be found easily on the internet—via search engines, on social media portals, and with voice search. And you should ensure that your company data are correct and up to date on every different portal where that data appears. Getting information to consumers is of no use if that information misleads them. (Refer to chapter 5 for more about the importance of having the right and correct data.)

In addition to presenting basic information about your company for searchers, you should also consider how to engage the interest of potential customers and motivate them to get in touch with you. You have to start with an analysis of the needs, desires, and pain points of the kind of consumers you want to attract. For example, if a hairdresser is targeting women in the age range during which women usually get married, the hairdresser could offer special and specially priced services for brides and bridesmaids. A hairdresser targeting older women could address issues around hair coloring, offer a hair coloring consultation, and provide an introductory offer for having hair colored. Businesses in other industries can make similar offers. A plumber targeting households in his neighborhood could address how to deal with clogged sewer pipes, dripping faucets, plumbing leaks, etc.

Once you have engaged a consumer's interest in your company, the next step is to collect their email address and offer a download of your app, if you have one. This provides a way for you to stay in touch with a consumer who is showing interest in what your company offers and is ripe for being turned into a buyer.

CASE STUDY:
LACANCHE

This study of how DexVille worked with Lacanche shows how defining all relevant **buyer personas** and a target group are preconditions for finding the exactly appropriate way to successfully talk to one's customers.

THE COMPANY

Ets. Abel Falisse is the exclusive importer of the brand Lacanche, which specializes in producing personalized, high-quality cooking pianos for gastronomes. Experience, craftsmanship, and innovation are united by Lacanche to offer chefs and culinary enthusiasts the tools that allow them to express their talents fully. Customer satisfaction and loyalty are their trademarks.

THE CHALLENGE

The challenge was to define, understand, segment and reach out to the potential target group of Lacanche. Ets. Abel Falisse also wanted to launch a specific activation campaign to generate leads and collect data.

THE SOLUTION

DexVille started by building a brand awareness strategy. They defined three brand buying personas and created a video targeted at each of these personas. Different, appropriate channels, such as YouTube, Facebook, and Instagram, were used to reach each persona and bring Lacanche products to top of mind and keep it there. Conversion was generated by leading the target groups to a dedicated landing page with a form to download the catalog and see the full range of possibilities that Lacanche offers. They put the focus on inspiring people who used a cooking piano and emphasized the reasons to choose Lacanche quality. To keep in contact with the leads, they set up an email follow-up. The first email included a catalog and offered a Lacanche distributor/dealer locator. The goal of the second email was to reactivate people after the catalog download with a **call to action**: discover our Lacanche showroom, and make an appointment with an advisor.

THE RESULT

The 739 emails sent achieved an opening rate of 38 percent, which is an excellent result compared to average opening rates between 20 and 30 percent.

TURNING LEADS INTO BUYING CUSTOMERS

To win the business of potential customers, you need to show how you can provide them with real value. For example, sharing examples of satisfied customers could be the hook that gets an interested consumer to commit to trying your products and services. A landscaper could display before-and-after pictures that show the results of his work—as could any business that provides transformative services such as hair styling, remodeling, auto bodywork, etc. And any kind of business can share quotes from satisfied customers on its website and point potential customers to positive reviews on the internet.

Another technique is to provide a free demonstration of your products and/or services. A free trial can convince a potential customer you are the right company to work with. And last, but not least, you need to make your basic pricing information available along with product features and the extent of the services you have available. Price may not be the ultimate determining factor in the consumer's decision, but they need to know what you can do for them and whether your products and services are within their price range.

MOTIVATING EXISTING CUSTOMERS TO BUY AGAIN AND BUY OTHER THINGS

It is a major mistake not to develop a relationship with your customer once your product or service is delivered and the invoice is paid. Some may look at the transaction as the *culmination* of a company's relationship with a customer, but it really ought to be just the *beginning*. Everybody who has bought a product on Amazon knows how it works. You will get emails from them at some point after your purchase, offering you a similar product. Also, at the bottom of the web page where you choose your product is a group of additional products under the headings "Frequently bought together" and "Products related to this item."

Amazon is smart enough to take advantage of their knowledge of what a customer likes, exemplified by what they are buying or considering buying, to offer other products that might interest them. For example, the landscaper who cuts a customer's lawn can offer services according to the seasons— pruning plants in autumn to get ready for winter, putting in new plantings in spring, etc. A restaurant can offer its regular customers a special menu and/or special pricing for a Valentine's Day supper or an Easter brunch. Possible ways to motivate your customers to return or to sell them additional products and services are limited only by your imagination.

> It is a major mistake not to develop a relationship with your customer once your product or service is delivered and the invoice is paid.

ASKING CUSTOMERS TO BE BRAND PROMOTERS

Ratings and reviews have become a potent marketing tool. It is simply a fact, now, that most consumers read ratings and reviews before making a purchase decision. Therefore, you should ask your satisfied customers to write reviews about their experience with your company. Please refer to chapter 8 for more details on how to get ratings and reviews and what to do with negative ones.

THE MOST IMPORTANT COMMUNICATION CHANNELS

You have to think of digital marketing as a spider web. Social media, blog posts, email marketing, direct marketing, and so on all work together as a network, delivering your content, your message, your brand to your prospects and customers in an incredible number of ways.

EMAIL: YOUR PREMIUM COMMUNICATION CHANNEL

Email is an important marketing tool. It has a higher ROI than most other channels, so it's essential to moving customers from one stage to the other in the **customer journey**. It is cost effective and doesn't have to take a lot of time.

It is also a good way to allow your customers to stay in touch with you, which enables you to demonstrate your expertise by giving them advice, helping them solve problems. Put your email address everywhere—letters, invoices, signs, etc.

Email is effective for a great variety of purposes.

New customers:

- Getting people to sign up for an event or a subscription.

- Following up on a subscription to welcome a new customer and introduce your brand.

- Explaining the benefits of working with your business.

- Explaining to customers what they can expect from working with you and what the next steps are for them to take advantage of your products and services.

Triggering purchases:

- Promoting a special offer, new product, or special event.

- Moving customers to the next stage of the **customer journey** by triggering new sales possibilities among segmented subscribers.

Retaining customers:

- Building and retaining a relationship with each of your customers by offering free content via a newsletter or a blog, as well as surveying customers to find out their needs and wants and get feedback on their experience with your business.

- Celebrating the anniversary of a customer's relationship with you or sending birthday congratulations, deepening your relationship.

- Following up on customer transactions with emails that include order confirmation, a receipt, a coupon, etc. Because emails have the highest open rate, they have to be carefully written, especially when they follow up a negative transaction (an unsubscribe, a product return, etc.). A complaint provides an opportunity to turn a negative into a positive with consumers *if* you follow up quickly and take good care of the complaining customer.

- Reengaging with those who have not bought anything from you in a long period of time.

But, because email is not ideal for everyone:

- Be very selective about the people you send it to.

- Send email newsletters only to subscribers who have given permission to receive emails.

- Send email promotions only to groups you think will be interested.

- Don't overdo it! Too many emails can be annoying to existing and prospective customers.

EMAIL MARKETING SOFTWARE

There are email management services you can hire to make sure your emails do not end up in spam folders, to check the **blacklist** status of any new email addresses, and to help you avoid big **bounce rates**. Many such services also offer:

- Automated email campaigns, with replies sent in response to those emails by prospects or customers: for example, a confirmation that you have received the email and will answer shortly, or you are currently out of the office and will take care of the email as soon as you return to the office.

- Professional reporting tools that show your emails' open rates and click-through rates, excluding people who opted out of receiving your emails.

- Mobile optimization to ensure that your emails can be read on mobile devices.

- Email address management, where opt-outs are unsubscribed from your mailing list, the address pool is constantly rechecked with a **blacklist** where people are listed who do not want to receive mails to avoid legal privacy problems, and address pools are created for special email campaigns.

WRITING SUCCESSFUL EMAILS

You need engaging subject lines to grab the attention of the person receiving your emails because it will take only a few seconds to decide whether or not to open an email. Those subject lines need to do the following:

- Make the recipient curious about the content of the email

- Hint at the benefit recipients will receive by opening the email

- Show deadlines for special offers

- Help your email avoid being buried in a spam folder by not using words that will get them automatically sent there, such as "No risk" / "Congratulations"/ "You won" / "Jackpot" / "XXX" / "For adults only" and so on

In addition to the subject line, many email programs show the first line or lines of an email in the inbox, so those are very important, too, and must do things similar to what the subject line does: arouse curiosity, demonstrate a benefit to the reader, make deadlines for special offers clear, and avoid spam trigger words. So you should consider the first paragraph of your email carefully because it is a highly important factor in whether or not your email is going to be read.

Other techniques that will make your emails more effective are:[34]

- Personally addressing the email recipient

- Making sure it's clear who sent the email, including your company's name and logo and even your name

- Clearly outlining the benefits to the recipient of your products and services

---

34   To learn more about making your emails effective, visit: Marvin Hintze, "16 Tips for Successful Email Marketing in 2021," Hubspot.de, January 8, 2021, accessed September 2021, https://blog.hubspot.de/marketing/email-marketing.

- Highlighting the **call to action (CTA)**

- Including interesting **links** for the recipient to follow

- Integrating engaging videos and animated GIFs

- Using a "PS" to emphasize your message or highlighting an additional topic

- Asking recipients for their thoughts on the subject matter of the emails

- Asking recipients to choose how frequently they want to receive your emails

There are also methods for optimizing your email campaigns:

- Running tests to determine which subject line will be more successful at getting recipients to open your email (known as **A/B testing**)

- Timing your emails well by testing to find out which is the best day of the week and time of day to send mails in order to get the best open rates

- Setting up a calendar that shows you when to send which mails for which reason or to achieve which goal

- Responding to inquiries, including complaints, in a timely manner

- Sending out your email to those who have not opened the first mail

MY SPECIAL ADVICE

Email marketing is strictly regulated by laws, and you must strictly obey those regulations in order to avoid fines. To achieve this:

- Provide a double-opt-in procedure. This means that, before adding a person to your subscription list, a person must:
  - First, agree to store their email address and to receive your emails
  - Second, respond to a confirmation email sent to their email address by clicking on the **link** in the confirmation email.

- Provide a privacy policy that users can read and indicate they accept.

- Include a statement about how you protect consumer data and about how you are storing and using the data, confirming that the data will not be given to or sold to a third party.

- The legal note must contain the contact data of the sender: company name, address, phone number, etc.

- Include an opt-out button in the email.

- Include a **link** to an unsubscribe page, where, after the recipient unsubscribes, you can confirm that their email address has been taken off your mailing list and will not be used anymore.

To avoid legal problems down the road, I recommend that you discuss your email template with your legal advisor before using it. There are actually attorneys who focus on finding shortcomings in email marketing approaches and suing senders on behalf of recipients! If you make a legal mistake in your email campaigns, the fees you'll have to pay your legal advisor will be only a small portion of the fines and damages you may have to pay.

CASE STUDY:
DHK

Here is an excellent example of how a mailing program with corresponding landing pages can be implemented on the basis of the **customer journey** in order to obtain high-quality leads.

THE COMPANY

DHK is specialized in the distribution of semifinished aluminum, stainless steel, and plastic products. They offer a wide choice of items to meet various applications and sectors of activity. Thanks to a wide range of services, DHK can provide tailor-made products fully in line with the standards and wishes of a customer.

THE CHALLENGE

The DHK group of Belgium turned to DexVille to generate better leads and a strategy for turning more of them into customers. DexVille started by building a lead-generating strategy for DHK. After collecting data of their B2B audience, they put focus on microconversions via brochure download per type of activity. As this was quite successful, generating an average of one thousand leads per month, DHK wanted to implement a lead qualification program. The challenge was to highlight qualified leads with high potential and to convert those leads into recurring clients.

THE SOLUTION

DexVille focused on marketing automation, enabling DHK to segment their leads and communicate with companies in a personalized and automated way. In order to capture DHK's needs and qualifying criteria, the agency started by organizing an internal workshop with DHK, facilitating the development of a personalized approach. Based on the insights from these workshops, they defined a nurturing flow with custom mail drip programs.

Leads were ultimately segmented into six sectors. For each sector, DexVille built a welcome scenario with specific content and timing. Step by step, the scenario allowed DHK to better understand a prospect's intentions. Following the request for one of the segmented brochures via an online form, DHK can now detect hot leads and follow up on relevant prospects.

THE RESULT

DHK's sales team has saved time, which allows them to provide a better and faster service to their most relevant prospects. With €3.98 average **cost-per-lead** and a 50 percent open rate for follow-up emails, this campaign has generated a high ROI.

CONTENT MARKETING

By giving good advice on suitable topics, blogs as part of your **content marketing** are a perfect way to strengthen your brand, attract new customers, and help keep customers loyal.

A blog can

- raise awareness of your business;

- position your company and/or yourself as an expert on the subject you are discussing in a given blog;

- win goodwill by helping consumers solve problems; and

- inspire, motivate, entertain, and convince prospective and existing customers.

When writing for existing or potential customers, it is important to know, and keep in mind, what you've learned about them and where they are in their **customer journey**. Blog posts are usually used at the beginning of the **customer journey** to raise awareness and to address cold prospects. But there is also something to be gained by addressing customers further along on their **customer journey**.

You need to work out a plan for your blog that defines:

- The goals you want to achieve with it.

- How to publish it (usually on your company's website).

- Its tone and style.

- What the content will be and when you will publish on each subject. (Your customer profiles should help you determine content: What do they want to know? Which problems and challenges are they facing? What objections might they have regarding your products and services? See chapters 1 and 2 for more on this subject.) If your competitors have blogs, see what subjects they write about and find your own slant on those subjects.

- Ways to repurpose the content you create, so you can get the most out of the effort you put into writing it. For example, regularly publishing on your website will refresh it, which makes it score higher in search algorithms. You can use the content in your email newsletter and **link** to the blog, and you can feature the content in social media and also **link** to your blog.

HOW TO OPTIMIZE A BLOG

Google Analytics will show you which blog posts receive the most traffic and where this traffic comes from. A blog post should include the possibility for the recipient to share the text in the recipient's social media channels. The easier it is to share a text, the more often it will be shared. The wider the reach, the better the standing in the community.

Using **search engine optimization (SEO)** writing techniques in your blogs will get you better rankings in search engines. (See the basics of **SEO** in chapter 4.) Cross-links to other sites or to blog authors who have written something related to the topic you are dealing with will give your audience even more help with their problems, demonstrating that you have their best interests at heart. You can say something like, "This could also be interesting for you" to introduce these cross-links. You can also **link** to relevant material on social media sites such as Facebook, LinkedIn, Twitter, etc.

Develop a certain time routine, template, style and distinctive voice for your blogs, so your users will develop a sense of who you are and what you have to offer them. It's also much more efficient to write a blog if you're not always reinventing things. You can also use videos and podcasts in your blog to make it more engaging. And ask your readers for feedback and comments to get them more involved.

HOW TO WRITE A BLOG

Some kinds of content that would work well on a business's blog are:

- Practical advice and solutions to problems. For example, a plumber could describe how to install a new drainpipe; a carpenter could describe how to protect furniture against woodworms; a fashion boutique could give recommendations on how to dress for special occasions or about new fashion trends, etc. Include helpful features, such as checklists of things to do and/or things not to forget.

- Insights into your company and how it works. For example, describing the origin of materials used in your products or how the stages of production yield excellent products; or highlighting employee expertise and achievements or awards your company has won.

- Customer success stories (always with their prearranged consent!) that demonstrate how customers have benefited from your products and services. For example, a dog trainer could describe turning an unruly dog into a safe family pet or a sporting goods store could talk about supplying a new youth football league with all of the equipment it needed.

- Reports on trade fairs and technical innovations that would be of interest to your customers and relevant to your business. For example, an electronics store could report on the latest innovations in flat-screen TVs or surround sound.

- Infographics that convey statistics in an easily understandable, visual way that relates to your customers' lives or businesses. For example, an HVAC company could include a graphic showing how temperatures have been and will continue to rise during the summer. Good and informative graphics have a high probability of being shared.

- Frequently asked questions (FAQs) and questions that should be asked. For example, a builder could list all the things a homeowner should take into account when planning to renovate a kitchen.

HAVE A STRONG HEADLINE

As with the subject line in an email, the headline of your blog (and subhead, if you have one) is highly important for engaging your audience's interest. A blog headline should:

- Be squarely aimed at the recipients' interests and goals and make the benefit of reading the blog clear: "How to Stay Healthy During Lockdowns."

- Pique the reader's curiosity: "Ten Ways to Stretch Your Monthly Budget."

- Ask a pertinent question: "Is Your Daily Milk Consumption Harming Your Health?"

- Provide and comment on news of interest: "How Google's Latest Changes in Website Rankings Affect You."

- All blogs should be written to prove your expertise—to your customers and prospects, as well as to Google.

MAKE IT EASY TO READ

Immediately after your engaging title, you need a strong introduction to catch the readers' interest and make them want to keep reading. And the content that follows should be easy to read, with simple words, short paragraphs, intertitles, bullet points, etc. Integrating pictures and videos can increase interest because the text alone can become boring to some people, but be aware of loading time because you'll lose readers if pictures and videos don't load quickly. And don't use agency pictures because they are widely available and much more likely to have been used elsewhere, so they are not unique. And unique photos support the Google ranking of your blog post.

When you write your blog post, be sure to fulfill the promise made in the headline. If you don't, readers will be frustrated and angry; they'll leave your blog and never come back!

Your **call to action (CTA)** should be clear and specific, and you should make it as easy as possible for the reader to take that action: "Call this number," "Email us here," "Bring in this coupon before November 10."

Finally, you need an effective conclusion that motivates readers to remember you, to read more of your blog posts, and to share your blog with colleagues and friends.

If you do not consider yourself a good writer, seek the help of a professional writer/editor to ensure that your blog has all of the good qualities outlined here. It's well worth the investment![35]

SOCIAL MEDIA

I'll say more about social media in chapter 8, but I want to introduce the subject here because social media are an important way of talking to your customers and potential customers. Similar to blogs, social media is a great channel for engaging with people, communicating about current trends/topics, raising awareness of your business, establishing your expertise with a target group, and promoting your products and services. Social media is a great place to tell your story (you can reuse blog material or other content you've created) and to have a dialogue with your customers and potential customers.

AUDIO AND VIDEO PODCASTS

Today, people tend to want to read less, preferring to listen to and view content. The advantage of spoken material is that it can be consumed on the go. People can hear what you have to say while they're driving or shopping or running or lying in bed. The advantage of video podcasts is that you can show people how to do things.

Podcasts can be fairly easily produced and distributed. As with any of these forms of communication, you need to plan what material

---

35 To learn more about blog writing for beginners, visit "How to Start a Blog in 2021," The BlogStarter.com, August 3, 2021, accessed September 2021, https://www. theblogstarter.com/.

you're going to share when and create a plan for doing it—and stick to that plan.

The advantages of audio podcasts are that they:

- present an opportunity to reach new target groups;

- are trusted by listeners to deliver authentic messages, not polished marketing messages;

- are really different from typical advertisements and marketing messages;

- can attract faithful followers if they provide good material that listeners like;

- can, with good planning and a consistent way of presenting, become a great and fairly cost-effective marketing tool;

- can give you access to people you wouldn't otherwise be able to reach—such as influencers in your area of business—by inviting them to be interview partners on your podcasts; and

- can be easily distributed as live streaming or offline download via different channels.

The advantages of video podcasts are that they:

- allow you to convince with both visual and audio messages;

- are effective at inspiring, entertaining, and informing audiences;

- have visual content that is more easily remembered;

- allow you to actually demonstrate a product online or present a "how to" tutorial;

- sometimes go viral, which audio alone is less likely to do;

- have descriptions, titles, and a level of quality that help them get better search rankings; and

- can easily be mobile-optimized.

You do, however, need to learn and follow the technical requirements for posting videos on sites such as YouTube.

HOW TO START PRODUCING AN AUDIO OR VIDEO PODCAST

After choosing audio or video podcasts as the channel to address your community, you have to set up a consistent content plan. This, like any form of marketing, starts with considering who your potential customers are and which topics might be of interest to them. You also need to investigate whether or not there are already podcasts that deal with these topics. If there are, you need to find a way to differentiate the information that you'll offer on your podcast.

After these basic preparations, you have to find a name for your podcast and design a cover that will characterize it appropriately online. You have to create the intro and outro files that will brand your podcast every time. With an audio podcast, it is essential to decide whether to offer it live streaming or as a download. With a video podcast, be sure it looks professional, with an appropriate background, illumination, sound, etc.—although there is no need to achieve Hollywood standards! You just don't want anything interfering with getting your message across or making you look unprofessional. In case this sounds too difficult, maybe one of your employees familiar with these media can help you, or you can ask an agency providing the basic settings enabling you to upload your files.

The next step is to outline the content for your podcast series. Each audio sequence should take no longer than twenty-five minutes, and video clips should be about six to ten minutes. Testing the release of the podcast at different times will eventually tell you which time is most appropriate for your community.

Because you are an expert in your field and know the pain points of your buyers, it should be relatively easy for you to define the topics you want to discuss in your podcast. The key is to be authentic and really help or entertain people, *not* trying too obviously to sell your products and services.

When you're ready to go, you can publish your audio files or videos on your website, your social media channels, YouTube, iTunes, Spotify, Google Play, and so on.[36]

MY SPECIAL ADVICE

There are (too) many channels available to reach out to your prospects and customers. Since it is simply not possible to use all of them, my advice about using them is:

- Choose wisely which channels you want to use—by learning which channels are best for reaching your target group.

- Consider well which channel you can use in a professional way that won't be tainted by too much surrounding visual "noise" or inappropriate content.

---

36 To learn more about producing a good podcast, check out chapter 8 to read more about videos, and visit the article "How to Make a Good Podcast" on Wikihow at https://www.wikihow.com/Make-a-Good-Podcast. Lower Street's article "How to Produce a Podcast: Quick & Easy Ways to Win Success" at https://lowerstreet.co/how-to/produce-a-podcast is a great resource as well, both accessed September 2021.

- Use channels that are easily available and work well on as many consumer devices as possible.

- Plan long-term, choosing channels that, once chosen, will enable you to commit to that channel for a long time.

- Do not try to put out content on too many platforms so that you find yourself putting more time into this than you really have available while running your business.

- Don't invest too much money in expensive technology or external support—keep control of how much you put out and how often you do it.

- If you have staff and one of them is especially familiar with a particular channel, ask that person to take responsibility for putting out material on that channel.

KEY TAKEAWAYS

- Know your customer and target audience profiles and use them!

- Know the different stages of the **customer journey** and where each of your customers is on that journey.

- Choose the appropriate content that will help move your customers from one stage of the journey to the next.

- Choose wisely the communication channels that are most suitable for your business and for distributing your content.

- Take advantage of the power that email communication delivers—if it is professionally implemented.

- Implement a blog to raise awareness of your business with potential customers and to help retain existing customers if your business provides enough qualified content.

- Choose wisely the social media that will help get your messages to your prospects and customers.

- Consider using video and audio podcasts to reach new target audiences. They need to be professional enough to be pleasant to watch or listen to (but not *expensively* professional); they need to be authentic and really help or entertain your community, *not* trying too obviously to sell your products and services.

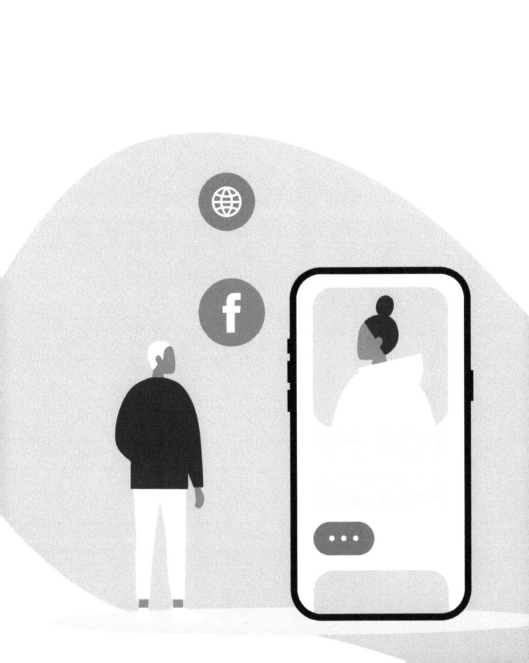

CHAPTER EIGHT

HOW TO TAKE THE MOST ADVANTAGE OF SOCIAL MEDIA

YOUR COMMUNICATION STRATEGY ON DIFFERENT CHANNELS

■   ■   ■

Social networks offer SMBs an affordable and efficient way to communicate with existing customers and acquire new ones—in a relatively simple way. Not so long ago, marketers would not even have dared to dream of such possibilities.

The April 2021 global report from DataReportal shows that there are 4.33 billion active social media users worldwide, increasing by more than 13.7 percent in the past twelve months.[37] Daily time spent with social media averages two hours and twenty-two minutes.

---

37   Simon Kemp, "Digital 2021 April Global Statshot Report," DataReportal, April 21, 2021, accessed July 20, 2021, https://DataReportal.com/reports/digital-2021-april-global-statshot.

There are countless social media platforms, all with their own processes and rules. The number of options may seem scary at first. But don't worry. Once you've decided on the appropriate and targeted platforms, it's not all that difficult. Social media marketing is also nothing more than a marketing method that helps you engage in a dialogue with customers and partners and interact with influencers. But just like in TV, radio, and print media, you have to pay for reach in social media. Do not get carried away and forget the cost.

WHAT WILL YOU DO ON THE PLATFORM?

Which social media platforms you use depends on your target group and what you intend to achieve on the platform. Basically, social media is about doing four things:

- Listening

- Networking

- Influencing

- Selling

Let's discuss each of these activities.

LISTENING

Social media platforms where users mainly interact with each other are perfect for listening to their dialogues and learning about and from them. Here, your customers and potential customers communicate with each other, and your competitors' customers communicate with each other, too. All you have to do is to listen! (But don't make the mistake of listening only on the internet! Listen to your customers in real life as well, asking them questions and taking notes.) It is possible to glean a lot of information about consumers' likes and dislikes by paying attention to what they say to one another about your industry.

NETWORKING

Social media channels are also good for networking. They allow you to stay in touch with current customers and get in touch with potential new customers. The most important so-called engagement channels are Facebook, Twitter, and LinkedIn—the latter for the B2B sector only. But you should also listen and network on Amazon, Yelp, and YouTube when people talk about your products there. Nowadays, users expect companies to pay attention to what is being said about the companies on the social web. It's best to view social media as another channel to serve your customers and a way to spread your good name. In the jargon, this is called "reputation management." If you listen, you'll also find out who's calling the shots on the social web in your industry and which influencers or journalists you would best network with.

INFLUENCING AND SELLING

Platforms that are employed by users in a similar way to search engines, when they want to find out about something or are looking for something, are particularly suitable for social influencing and selling. YouTube and Pinterest are good examples of this type. If users search for your topic area here, they *must* be able to find your content.

Through your social media activities, you can create trust for your brand, which will make it easier for you to sell to consumers. People trust their friends, and that's a fact you can take advantage of here. If your content is so interesting that users share it, they will be showing it to their friends, and those friends will trust their recommendation, and your posts will make the rounds, creating awareness of your company and attracting customers.

The 2021 Shopper Experience Index by Bazaarvoice is a study of selling on social media. It revealed that:[38]

> Overall, about one in three shoppers globally have made a purchase on social media in the past year. But when you break it down by age, that number climbs to 43% of eighteen-to-twenty-four-year-olds and 47% of twenty-five-to-thirty-four-year-olds. While less common with shoppers thirty-five and older, buying on social media has become as common as "liking" a post online. The most popular platforms for making a purchase are Facebook, Instagram, and YouTube, according to a visual user-generated content survey we conducted in 2021. Shoppers say they buy this way because they like how the products look in a brand or retailer's post (31%), followed by it being easy (27%). Part of the way brands and retailers can make buying on social media easy is by tagging the product itself in a post, and 38% of shoppers say this makes them more likely to click, click, buy on a social post.

WHAT TO CONSIDER

The most important question to ask yourself in all your social media activities is: What is relevant? If you let this guide you, the decision as to whether a topic or posting is appropriate or not will be answered quite simply. You need to determine:

---

38   Bazaarvoice, "2021 Shopper Experience Index: Rethinking the Approach to Retail," accessed July 20, 2021, https://media.bazaarvoice.com/Shopper-Experience-Index-2021-ebook-EN.pdf.

What is really relevant ...

- for my target group?

- for conveying my core message?

- to achieve my defined goals?

For example, a **call to action** without any context is definitely out of place on social media. As with other channels, you need a clear concept here as well. You need to know who you are, what you want to convey, and how you're going to determine if you're succeeding at getting your message across. The clarity this creates will make your ongoing work much easier.

THE IMPORTANCE OF SOCIAL MEDIA FOR BOOSTING YOUR GOOGLE RANKING

Google likes it when companies are represented on social media and actively spread their messages there, and that is an important consideration. If users then also appreciate your posts through likes, comments, and shares, this has a positive effect on your ranking factor on Google. This means that you increase your chances of being found on search engines for **keywords** relevant to your business.

THE ABILITY TO MEASURE YOUR SUCCESS

In social media, you can constantly get an overview of what level of success your individual actions have brought. You will know exactly how often a post has been viewed, liked, or shared and what the interaction rate looks like. With this knowledge, you not only have transparency about the results of your efforts, but you can also respond to this information by optimizing your advertising activities through better targeting.

Most important of all, however, is that you are available on social platforms for your customers and prospects and that you convey a clear, strong message there about your business.

WHICH CHANNELS SHOULD YOU USE?

Which platforms you use depends on your target groups and what they are up to. It's best to first find out which networks your customers use, follow them, and engage in a dialogue with them. If your resources are tight, start with just one or two channels. You can then add more channels, little by little.

> Most important of all, however, is that you are available on social platforms for your customers and prospects and that you convey a clear, strong message there about your business.

In any case, the decision about which platforms you deliberately leave out is one of the most important of all. After all, you don't want to get bogged down and put in a lot of effort that has little or no effect on your business or doesn't sufficiently contribute to the goals you've defined for this activity. However, on some portals, it does make sense to be present mainly for the **SEO** reasons I've mentioned previously (please refer to chapter 5 regarding the need to be present anytime and anywhere).

Global usage of social media is incredibly strong. Apart from messenger services such as WhatsApp, for almost 22 percent of global internet users aged sixteen to sixty-four, Facebook is the favorite social media platform, followed by Instagram with 18.4 percent and Twitter with nearly 5 percent.[39]

---

39   Simon Kemp, "Digital 2021 April Global Statshot Report."

The major social media platforms include:

- Facebook

- Instagram

- YouTube

- WhatsApp

- Twitter

- TikTok

- Snapchat

- Pinterest

- LinkedIn

Let's look at each of these platforms.

FACEBOOK

When you consider that there are around 1.8 billion active users on Facebook every day (308 million in Europe) and that 3.3 billion people use the platform's services at least once a month, it quickly becomes clear that this is an extremely powerful marketing tool.[40]

Of course, almost every company wants to be part of it. But many approach marketing on Facebook "actionistically," almost in the same way they use social media platforms privately. As I mentioned previously, there's no use just posting for the sake of posting. If the posts are not relevant to your target group, you will not generate any likes and—even worse—you'll *lose* your fan or subscriber base. Rebuilding such a base is quite a tedious and time-consuming process.

---

40 Philipp Roth, "Nutzerzahlen: Facebook, Instagram, Messenger und WhatsApp, Highlights, Umsätze, uvm," AllFacebook.de, April 29, 2021, accessed September 2021, https://allfacebook.de/toll/state-of-facebook.

Also, it is very important to remember that social media users' personal profiles may only be used by private individuals and only for private purposes. Companies can create a Facebook page and declare themselves as a local business, a company, an organization, an institution, or a brand or product, but a legal note must be included on the organization's page.

In order to proceed in a targeted manner—a manner that is much more likely to be effective—you should create a content plan tailored to your company and your target audience.

Ask yourself what you want your Facebook site to do for you. Do you want to:

- Chat with customers?

- Tell stories about your brand?

- Promote your products? (And, if so, which products and in what doses?)

Once you've established these things, you'll also quickly know what your posts need to look like and what content has no place on your site.

FOLLOWERS, FOLLOWERS, FOLLOWERS …

One thing you must *always* keep in mind: If you don't have followers, your unpaid actions on Facebook will be pointless. Therefore, use all your marketing and communications channels (offline as well as online) to publish **links** to your social media presences: on your website, in emails, and on folders and other print advertising materials. Also, use the contacts you have made in your private Facebook presence and invite them to follow your company page.

And be aware that your Facebook posts will not be seen by all your followers. The truth is that if you are not paying for greater reach, only a fraction of your followers will see them. Reach is not free on social media. If you want to draw more attention to your Facebook site or your offers on social media, you will have to pay for it. But that investment can certainly be worthwhile if that reach is well targeted.

PLACING ADVERTISEMENTS

When you run ads on Facebook, they are displayed for your defined target audience. However, keep in mind that ads can interrupt the user in what he or she actually wants to do on Facebook—namely, to find out what friends are up to. Advertisements should therefore be designed in such a way that the user enjoys them, rather than feeling bothered by them. And ads should only be displayed to the appropriate target group, people who are really interested in the content.

The Facebook Ad Manager, through which you can place ads, is user friendly and relatively easy to use. When creating a campaign, you can set the goal of the campaign. There are many options to choose from, such as driving traffic to your website or getting views of your videos. Then you can choose your target groups. It's best to think of the unique **buyer personas** you have defined and consider what brands, personalities, events, books, etc., might interest them. Who do you want to target? Where do you want them to be directed, or what do you want them to do? It is the answers to these most important questions that will determine whether your Facebook ads will be successful.

Of course, the impact and language of the messages you put out are also important. Address the problem that your products will solve for consumers, removing any doubts they might have about your products and services and delivering a clear **call to action**.

The costs for advertising on Facebook are not extreme, so you can easily take some first steps and try them out, even with small money. If you don't want to dive into targeting and buying ads yourself, a social media agency will be happy to do it for you. (For example, my own company, FCR Media, works out social media campaigns for businesses, primarily on Facebook, Instagram, and YouTube, based on hundreds of criteria ranging from regional and demographic aspects to interests and behavior.)

> **Address the problem that your products will solve for consumers, removing any doubts they might have about your products and services and delivering a clear call to action.**

INSTAGRAM

Instagram is a social network that thrives on images and videos, with a decidedly younger target group than Facebook. With its 1,287 million users per month, it is another particularly important social media platform for companies, alongside Facebook.[41] Instagram is generally used from a mobile phone and is therefore well suited to support your mobile strategy.

Text plays a subordinate role on Instagram. You first need interesting, appealing photos that generate attention or emotion in users. Admittedly, it will be easier for companies in the lifestyle or food sector to find such images than it will be for companies selling paper shredders or rain barrels. But good image stories can be found for any product if you try to think a little differently and look for creative ideas. For example, the rain barrel company could show images of nice-looking barrels beside houses and graphics that show how much water is preserved by using a rain barrel.

---

41   Simon Kemp, "Digital 2021 April Global Statshot Report."

Even if Instagram seems to be "just" about pretty pictures, it's important to develop a strategy about how to use it and to think carefully about the target audience you want to address through this medium and what your presence on Instagram should do for your business. It's best to follow your competitors on Instagram as well. This will give you an idea of relevant topics and images in your industry and suggest possible strategies and target groups—ones that are differentiated from those of your competitors.

To get started, you need to create a business account on Instagram. You can have a normal account converted into a business account for free. Once you start posting, via Insights, you can learn how many people each post has reached. And you have the opportunity to promote your posts and thus reach more users. Advertising on Instagram can be handled via the Facebook Ad Manager.

Another important reason to make yourself a content plan is because you should be active multiple times a week. The Insta-Algorithmus loves regular postings, so post a minimum of three times per week! Post stories, live streams, or video formats like IGTV or Reels—try out the different formats to find out which ones work best for what you want to convey.

On Instagram, you can't **link** from your posts directly to your website or landing page, like you can on Facebook. However, you can direct the user to the appropriate landing pages via a **link** in your bio. Outside of the bio, a direct **link** is only possible in paid ads.

Instagram categorizes content based on hashtags (#) to get it to appropriate users. Therefore, research well which hashtags will fit your company, products, and services and which will bring visitors to your business profile. Don't just use the really popular hashtags, but also use niche topic hashtags appropriate to your target audience. With the very popular hashtags, your material runs the risk of getting lost.

To generate users, you should also refer to your Instagram profile as often as possible on your website, in emails, on folders, roll ups, posters, etc.—any kind of consumer communication you put out.

YOUTUBE

Using video content has long since become a matter of course—especially for younger target groups—and you should use it if you have the time and inclination. Netflix, Sky, and Amazon Prime saved us from too much boredom during the pandemic, and during that period, they attracted vast numbers of new users to video content.

Whether it's cooking demonstrations, repair instructions, workout programs, or almost anything else you can imagine, videos have been growing in popularity for years. No matter what it is you don't know or need help with, enter it in a YouTube search, and you'll get access to countless videos with the tips or explanations you are looking for. YouTube has become the second-largest search engine after Google. It's a free platform, which is financed by advertising, currently registers over two billion logged-in users per month, and those users watch over a billion hours of video and generate billions of views![42]

Whether you're an international market leader, a start-up, or a small local business, and no matter what your industry, YouTube can be effective as a marketing channel. Many entrepreneurs are afraid of high costs when it comes to creating video content. But what you offer doesn't have to be a costly video produced by an agency. Quite the opposite! On YouTube, you score with viewers through authenticity and commitment. Good content that benefits the viewer is much

---

42   YouTube About, "YouTube in Numbers," accessed July 20, 2021, https://www.youtube.com/intl/en-GB/about/press/.

more decisive than the quality of the videos—although, of course, a decent quality should be delivered so that watching the video is a pleasant experience for the viewer. (See chapter 7 for more on using videos in podcasts.)

But before you set out to record videos and make YouTube an important cornerstone of your online presence, you should define your goals for this platform as well, determine which target group you want to address there, and think about how you can best showcase your company, your brand, and your products or services via videos. There are several basic types of videos that can be effective:

- Introductory

- Explanatory

- Customer interviews

INTRODUCTORY VIDEOS

With introductory videos, you can, in just a few minutes, give your audience an impression of who they are dealing with, what your expertise is, what you sell, and what benefits you can provide for your customers. When you make such a video, I strongly advise you not to just memorize text and recite it; instead, speak as authentically as possible from your real-life experience. This is an opportunity to introduce yourself and your company to potential customers and tell them your story. Try to approach the whole thing with humor and offer the viewer surprising elements that will capture their interest in who you are and what you do. This is where your creativity and that of your employees are needed, so get people involved who have good ideas and a sense of humor.

If you still need the motivation to get yourself in front of a camera, consider the fact that if you, as the head of the organization, present your company and your products in the introductory video, it will create trust in viewers and generate a positive emotional response. And for consumers, that is a good basis for making a decision to purchase from a company.

EXPLANATORY VIDEOS

Complex content, products, or services can be described in a clear and entertaining way with the help of an explanatory video. Such a video should provide answers to questions that potential customers would be concerned about. A video with a good explanation of how your products and services work—and most importantly, how they will benefit a customer—will help consumers overcome any uncertainties they might have about who you are and what you do.

It is not always necessary to feature the head of the company. You also can use another employee or an animated character. But make sure the imagery, colors, and style match your brand. Many companies offer the service of creating animated explanatory videos in different price ranges.

CUSTOMER INTERVIEWS

Nothing convinces potential buyers more than hearing from satisfied customers. (You can read more about this below when I talk about referral marketing.) You may already be making use of this in a brochure or company folder, including relevant quotes there. But why not record a video as well? It's much more intimate and personal than words on a page. Ask satisfied customers to allow you to interview them about their experiences with your company and your products. You will benefit doubly if you ask questions that customers frequently ask you and have them refute objections that you often encounter. This creates greater certainty in consumers and makes it easier for you to win new customers.

By default, YouTube plays advertising that fits the theme in the video it accompanies. However, since you certainly do not want to accidentally redirect your customers to your competitors, I recommend that you block advertising on your channel. To do this, check the box "Disable interest-based advertising." If you select this option, personalized ads will no longer be displayed within the videos on your channel.

It is also a great strategy to include all of your YouTube videos, or **links** to them, on your company website and in your blog and electronic newsletters. The more you distribute the videos through your channels, the greater the reach they will achieve.

If you want to advertise on YouTube and run promotional videos or ads, you can do that through Google Ads. It's the same platform because both platforms belong to American Alphabet, Inc.

WHATSAPP

With at least two billion active users, WhatsApp is the most popular messenger service and ranks third among the most used social media platforms after Facebook and YouTube. No wonder more and more companies are using it to address mobile users.[43] WhatsApp is best suited for keeping in touch with existing customers and advising them. When someone entrusts a company with a mobile number, it shows special interest in the company and its products. But what they certainly don't want is to be spammed with advertising at that number!

SMBs that are considering marketing on WhatsApp can download the WhatsApp Business app from their app store. It allows automated messages to be sent and chat statistics to be called up.

---

43   Simon Kemp, "Digital 2021 April Global Statshot Report."

In order for you to communicate with customers via the Messenger service, those customers need to add your mobile number to their contacts. This brings you very close to them and enables you to support them by answering everyday questions, putting yourself literally at their fingertips. This kind of accessibility strengthens your relationship with them.

The benefit of being this close to customers is that they are more likely to respond to your approaches. WhatsApp logs response rates of up to 95 percent! This is an enormously high rate, considering that in email marketing, even 20 to 30 percent is considered a great success.[44]

Whether a customer has a problem with a product, wants to know details about it, or wants to buy something, via WhatsApp, you can respond immediately, offer a solution, and satisfy them. Such straightforward service has a positive impact on customer loyalty and your company's image. And don't forget that people who are served well and quickly are happy to tell others about it!

Besides the standard features of sending and receiving text and voice messages, pictures, and videos, there are additional features. You can:

- Establish a company profile with contact data and pictures

- Send automated messages of greeting, notice of absence, etc.

- Prepare prewritten messages for FAQs

- Create chat labels to give you a better overview of chats

---

44   Matthias Mehner, "8 Kennzahlen, auf die Du im Messenger Marketing achten solltest!" Messengerpeople, March 23, 2018, accessed July 20, 2021, https://www.messengerpeople.com/de/8-kennzahlen-auf-die-du-im-messenger-marketing-achten-solltest/.

LEGAL FRAMEWORK

As with email marketing, it is important that your WhatsApp marketing adhere to the legal framework and proceed in a GDPR-compliant manner. With the standard double-opt-in procedure, you are on the safe side. Sending mass newsletters via WhatsApp is expressly prohibited. (For more on this, refer to chapter 7 on email marketing.)

TWITTER

On the microblogging platform Twitter, you can post text (tweets) with a maximum length of 280 characters. These can be shared (retweeted) by other users. For some time now, tweets with a photo have also been possible. As with Instagram, hashtags are what delineate areas of interest on Twitter.

Twitter has 396 million active users worldwide.[45] It is best suited for direct customer contact. If you are outgoing and responsive and contribute to problem-solving via your tweets, you can position yourself as an expert. However, if you have nothing substantive to say, nothing that will benefit Twitter users interested in your subject area, you won't succeed there. Added value for the user determines your success here even more than on other platforms.

Twitter users are the bold and cool ones, the ones who like to discover new things first. That's exactly what makes the platform attractive for companies. You can draw attention to your topic here with ads and use interest-based targeting to address the right target groups. So-called "promoted tweets" are displayed to users who have indicated an interest in a particular product or service, even if they do not follow your company directly.

---

45   Simon Kemp, "Digital 2021 April Global Statshot Report."

TIKTOK

The short video app TikTok is particularly suitable for companies and brands that want to address a young target group, especially Generation Z (born between 1995 and 2010).

The app has 732 million active users.[46] It is based on videos with a maximum length of three minutes. Thanks to its numerous functions, TikTok allows users to quickly make creative videos and accompany them with trendy music.

Anyone who succeeds in making inspiring videos can achieve great reach here—even with a small account.

It is by no means about perfection with these TikTok videos, but much more about uniqueness and authenticity. However, and this should be borne in mind, you are competing there with the videos of a very creative, young target group that's looking to have fun.

As with Instagram and Twitter, hashtags are used to filter which messages people receive by their areas of interest. Often the hashtag #foryou is used to increase the likelihood of getting to the "For You Page," a **home page** of sorts put together individually for each user. Branded hashtag challenges are often used to introduce a brand to potential new customers and to create awareness.

SNAPCHAT

You can also find Generation Z on Snapchat. DataReportal reports 528 million active users as of April 2021.[47]

On Snapchat, users can create and edit video- and photo-based stories and send them to friends. The content either disappears immediately after viewing or is deleted after twenty-four hours, at the latest.

---

46   Simon Kemp, "Digital 2021 April Global Statshot Report."

47   Simon Kemp, "Digital 2021 April Global Statshot Report."

With the so-called Memories and Share functions, content that users find particularly interesting can be archived and forwarded to friends. In this way, individual snaps can reach additional groups of users.

Marketers are often critical of the fact that content usually disappears quickly. But isn't that an argument *in favor* of Snapchat? Because of the short availability, users naturally pay a lot of attention to these so-called "Snaps." In addition, the transience creates a certain "live" quality that can help to increase the credibility of a brand.

Companies can use the discover page to place photos as well as videos and advertisements on Snapchat. For many companies targeting the young demographic, Snapchat has already become a permanent fixture in the marketing mix and an important tool for image building.

PINTEREST

The image search engine Pinterest, which has 459 million active users, works similarly to Google, except that it's all about images.[48] Users are looking for inspiration and new ideas. On their pinboards, they collect images and graphics that they like. These "Pins" are linked to websites and can be commented on. However, the focus on Pinterest is not on communication, and the number of followers does not play as big a role as on Facebook or Instagram.

Pinterest is particularly suitable for companies that have appealing images or sell products or services that can be well staged. In order for a presence on Pinterest to make sense for a company, a company needs to post regularly and provide its images with **keywords** for which it wants to be found. You should not expect quick success on Pinterest. It can take a few months before significant momentum is created.

---

48   Simon Kemp, "Digital 2021 April Global Statshot Report."

LINKEDIN

With about 756 million members, LinkedIn is the world's most widely used business network, even though it is not known how many are active every day.[49] It is mainly used to build professional networks and support people in their professional advancement. That is why it's an excellent place for companies in the B2B sector to do their marketing.

LinkedIn works completely differently from Facebook and Instagram. Here, it's not about product advertising or lead generation but about demonstrating expertise and communicating milestones, important happenings, and events at companies. It is a great place to strengthen B2B brands or do personal branding. And, of course, LinkedIn is also very useful if you are looking for new employees—not only by searching for them on the app but by attracting them to your company by the way you portray it and its accomplishments.

HOW TO

On LinkedIn's "About Us" page, you can place a description of your company and update it continuously. On so-called focus pages, which can be added, you can give details about individual business units, products, services, etc. The messages, articles, and other material you post will appear in the "Updates" section.

If you have a lot to say about a topic and want to promote it for yourself or your company, you can create a group on LinkedIn. But when you do this, you also take on the task of setting rules, monitoring and moderating posts, and getting conversations going—by, for

---

49   Mansoor Iqbal, "LinkedIn Usage and Revenue Statistics (2021)," BusinessofApps. com, July 5, 2021, accessed September 2021, https://www.businessofapps.com/ data/linkedin-statistics/.

example, throwing questions into the room. But it can be worth the effort, for when a new post is published on the group's page, all group members will receive a notification and will be reminded of your topic again and again.

Analytics available on each post will help you figure out which topics are interesting to users and bring the most interactions. If you sponsor posts, you'll achieve more reach there too.

SOCIAL MEDIA MONITORING

There are a number of excellent tools for social media monitoring, but most of them cost quite a bit of money. If you don't have the budget for this, you can use Google Alerts and search for your **keywords** every now and then via Google search. When searching for **keywords**, it's best to enter them into Google with question marks because this enables a broader search, which not only finds the exact **keyword** but related terms.

Hootsuite is a good tool for social media monitoring. With it, you can monitor the most important social media platforms such as Facebook, Instagram, YouTube, Twitter, and LinkedIn for a relatively low monthly cost, to see if your **keywords** are mentioned there.[50]

---

50   To learn more about social media monitoring, read "8 of the Best Social Media Monitoring Tools to Save You Time" on hootsuite.com, accessed September 2021, https://blog.hootsuite.com/social-media-monitoring-tools/.

MY SPECIAL ADVICE

Due to the popularity and reach of social media, it is hard to imagine a marketing mix without them. However, they do have their pitfalls. Poorly used, they can cause problems. Therefore, I strongly recommend that you avoid the mistakes listed below. Just doing this can make a big difference in the success of your social media presence.

BIGGEST SOCIAL MEDIA MISTAKES

- Ignoring conversations about your company or its products on social media

- Posting haphazardly and with a **call to action** that doesn't have any context

- Not communicating in a platform-compliant manner

- Communicating not personally but automatically and impersonally

- Only wanting to sell, not communicate

- Focusing on quantity over quality

- Not monitoring and responding to comments

- Deleting negative comments

- Posting too irregularly

- Using too many hashtags

- Leaving out **calls to action**

REFERRAL MARKETING FOR SMBS

In addition to recommendations from family and friends, ratings and reviews also influence consumers when purchasing a product or service. This influence was strengthened during the COVID-19 pandemic. A study of US consumers showed that 87 percent of them read online reviews for local businesses in 2020—up from 81 percent in 2019.[51]

Consumers are relying more and more on reviews when it comes to using a service, booking a hotel room, planning a visit to a restaurant, or buying a day cream, mobile phone, lawn mower, or any other product. There is hardly an area of business in which customer reviews do not already play an important role. However, the business segments where reviews are most frequently consulted and taken into account are restaurants, hotels, medical services, automotive shops, and clothing stores.

Despite this, many companies do not have so-called "recommendation marketing" on their radar—although it is inexpensive and does not require a great deal of effort—or they are only aware of it to an insufficient extent.

Consumers love to be reassured that they are making a good decision via reviews before buying online or even locally in a store. In the shopper experience index of 2021, the value of collecting ratings and reviews to increase sales is further explained:[52]

When shopping on a brand or retailer's website, almost 40% of shoppers won't purchase if there isn't User Generated Content

---

51 Rosie Murphy, "Local Consumer Review Survey 2020," BrightLocal, December 9, 2020, accessed July 20, 2021, https://www.brightlocal.com/research/local-consumer-review-survey/.

52 Bazaarvoice, "2021 Shopper Experience Index: Rethinking the Approach to Retail," accessed July 20, 2021, https://media.bazaarvoice.com/Shopper-Experience-Index-2021-ebook-EN.pdf.

(UGC) on the product page they're on. It's time to take what customers share with you on social media and go big with it.

48% of shoppers are reading reviews more now than they were before the pandemic. Reviews are still crucial for shoppers heading in-store, with 63% saying they're researching online before heading in-store.

Google also loves reviews and will thank you with a better **SEO** ranking if you eagerly collect those reviews because reviews offer added value for the user who is searching. Via the stars that are displayed with the Google entry of a company, it is immediately apparent to searchers how satisfied customers are with a provider.

Besides stars and written reviews, pictures are very helpful, as Bazaarvoice reports: "Recent studies show that besides written reviews photos included by customers even more increase the credibility of a review."[53]

So actively approach your satisfied customers, and ask them for reviews on portals relevant to your company. When customers are in your shop or office for a longer period of time, you may be able to hand them an iPad to enter their rating immediately, so they don't forget to do it when they get home. With your most loyal customers, you might take it a further step and encourage them to post videos about your service on social media. For example, a dog groomer could encourage clients to produce little video clips of their darling dogs after they've been groomed. These very loyal customers might also be willing to counter a negative review that appears, contrasting their experience with the negative reviewer's experience.

You could also give the customer a printed reminder and/or send them an email reminder. In addition, a request for reviews should be

53   Bazaarvoice, *A Picture's Worth a Thousand Purchases: How Visual and Social Content Increase Online Sales*, accessed July 20, 2021, https://www.bazaarvoice.com/resources/how-visual-and-social-content-increase-online-sales-research-report/.

included in each email sent after a purchase is completed or a product is delivered. It is crucial that you constantly get new reviews because only the most recent ones get the attention of potential customers. It is also crucial that you respond in a timely manner to new reviews, positive or negative.

DON'T BE AFRAID OF NEGATIVE REVIEWS

Negative reviews give many businesspeople a stomachache. However, they are not a problem if there are also good ones—and, in fact, a few negative reviews can even increase the credibility of the reviews overall. The decisive factor is the proportion of positive reviews to negative reviews. It is quite natural that not everything goes perfectly for a business, and consumers understand this.

But it *is* important that you respond quickly to negative reviews and do not leave them out there unanswered. Offer a constructive solution to people who post negative reviews. Listen carefully to what the customer disliked, and make sure you address it in your response. This is not only good for your reputation on the internet, but if handled well, it also can enable you to establish a good customer relationship with the negative reviewer, turning around that customer's attitude about your company. If you look at it from this perspective, negative reviews won't upset your stomach anymore. Over time, you will see them as valuable feedback that will help you to optimize your products and services.

If a customer raises an issue that cannot be resolved in a one-paragraph response, I recommend that you continue the dialogue via email—without the whole community watching and reading along. You can ask the person complaining to send you an email and say that you will respond immediately to take care of the problem. Potential customers will see this and realize that you are taking the customer's complaint seriously.

If a customer's review really makes you angry, take a deep breath, and don't respond to the customer who is complaining, but focus on the problem and respond calmly, objectively, and constructively.

And don't delete any negative reviews because that can backfire! Such an approach increases the dissatisfaction of angry customers, and they will definitely find space elsewhere to express their displeasure. Sometimes customers even take screenshots of their reviews and circulate them on the web, which can cause significant damage to your reputation.

MANY RATING PORTALS

There are now lots of rating portals on the internet: general ones, such as Google Business Profile, Yelp, ProvenExpert, or Facebook, and those specializing in specific industries. For example, for doctors, there are Jameda, DocInsider, or Sanego; for restaurants, there is Quando; and for hotel reservations, there are Booking.com, Tripadvisor, and HolidayCheck. Then there is Trusted Shops, which is about the safety of customers when shopping online. If the Trusted Shops seal of approval appears on your website, your store is likely to be considered trustworthy.

You can get quite stressed about keeping track of all this, but with special tools like Yext and Uberall, which I discussed in chapter 5, it's actually quite easy to do this. You will be informed as soon as a rating is received on one of the portals. And you can send an appropriate response to the review directly from these tools. This makes rating management much easier, and you never again have to be uncertain about whether you might have overlooked an important review on one of the numerous essential portals out there.

By the way, you should also answer the *positive* reviews, even if it is only with a short "Thank you for your feedback!" Those customers are doing you an important service and deserve to be thanked for it.

It also makes sense to integrate your reviews into your website because they contribute significantly to increasing your conversion rate.

MY SPECIAL ADVICE

Ratings and reviews should be a focus of your business on a daily basis. Provided you manage them in a smart way, they can definitely support your success.

My basic advice about dealing with customer feedback is this:

- Collect positive reviews.

- Say thank you for positive reviews.

- Keep calm in case of negative reviews.

- Take criticism/complaints seriously, and learn from them for the future.

- Answer criticism/complaints as quickly as possible and offer a solution.

- Always remain friendly and appreciative.

NET PROMOTER SCORE

A special form of referral marketing is the net promoter score (NPS). The NPS indicates to what extent a customer is willing to recommend a company, a product, or service. On a scale from 0 (very unlikely) to 10 (extremely likely), the customer is asked to define willingness to recommend the company to others. Those who respond from 0 to 6 are so-called "detractors," and those who choose from 9 and 10 are "promoters," while the answers from 7 to 8 are considered as being "indifferent" and are not included in the calculation. To finally calculate the NPS, the promoters are deducted from the detractors. The formula is:

$$\text{NPS} = \text{Promoters (in \% of all respondents)} - \text{Detractors (in \% of all respondents)}$$

While the NPS plays a big role in many companies for identifying overall customer satisfaction, there are definitely shortcomings to this score. The exclusion of the "indifferent" group is particularly criticized because many consumers are reluctant to give the highest scores to any company. For them, an evaluation of 7 and 8 is rather good, but according to the NPS calculation scheme, their ratings are not counted at all. The result is a tendency to poor results which do not reflect the real situation.[54]

---

54   To learn more about NPS, go to "What is NPS? Your ultimate guide to Net Promoter Score in 2021" at Qualtrics, accessed September 2021, https://www.qualtrics.com/experience-management/customer/net-promoter-score/.

INFLUENCER MARKETING

On average, 21.3 percent of worldwide internet users aged sixteen to sixty-four follow influencers or other experts on social media. Women follow them more than men, and the younger people are, the fonder they are of influencers.[55]

Influencer marketing refers to individuals who regularly publish online content and very often cooperate with companies to promote their products and services. Influencers can be celebrities, journalists, or bloggers who have managed to entertain a huge number of followers that regularly listen to them, view their content, and adopt the behavior of the influencer. One might think that the bigger the number of followers, the more impact the influencer has. But this is not necessarily the case. Sometimes influencers with a smaller number of followers can create an even stronger relationship with those followers, and therefore influence their followers more strongly than the very well-known influencers.

Typically, influencers are paid according to their reach or based on their activities. Whatever their arrangement is, they do have to clearly differentiate their private opinions from paid promotions of products and services.

If you think that influencer marketing could be effective for promoting your products and services, you should take advantage of these marketing experts that influence your area of business.

In Belgium, there is an interesting portal, https://nonon.world/, which motivates people to take part in so-called challenges for certain products and services. After registering, people can participate in the challenge and promote the brand on their own social profiles. Based on their reach and creativity, they are rewarded with free products.

---

55   Simon Kemp, "Digital 2021 April Global Statshot Report."

The companies benefit from the reach and awareness they achieve in multiple social media channels. Through this portal, virtually every social media user can act as an influencer.

CASE STUDY:
XERIUS/SD WORX

How can you inspire young people to become accountants? The best way is to get them to provide that inspiration to their peers. This is exactly why Xerius and SD Worx turned to influencer marketing and the agency NO-NON, a subsidiary of DexVille.

THE COMPANIES

Xerius is a business counter and a social insurance fund for the self-employed and entrepreneurs.

They partnered with SD Worx, an HR company that delivers people solutions across the entire employee lifecycle, "from paying employees to attracting, rewarding and developing the talent who make businesses succeed."

THE CHALLENGE

Both brands wanted to target possible future accountants to make accountancy careers and their accountancy training program top of mind in this youthful segment.

THE SOLUTION

The approach was to work with young nano- and microinfluencers (with one thousand to fifty thousand followers). These influencers are extremely valuable because they are perceived as neutral, honest, and fairer than the macro- and megacontracted influencers. NO-NON is a platform that connects these types of influencers with brands. On the NO-NON site, brands post challenges so that "NO-NON-fluencers" can take on the challenge and share creative content about the brand. The Xerius/SD Worx hope was that these influencers would show their peers that the existing prejudices about accountancy as a career were invalid. They got these influencers to post on this subject by offering a Cool-Blue coupon worth € 250 for the three best (greatest reach / most creative) posts.

THE RESULT

Sixteen thousand unique young users read and shared the NO-NON influencer posts about accountancy careers, including its being shared with the biggest high school group in Flanders.

KEY TAKEAWAYS

- Social media channels offer an enormous variety of possibilities for communicating with customers and prospects.

- Use professional tools to ensure that you know what is said about your company and your products or services on the web.

- Respond as promptly as possible to comments that concern you—whether they are positive or negative.

- Think carefully about which social media channels you want to actively use for your marketing, based on your insights about what the best channels are for meeting your kind of customers and prospects.

- Once you have made a decision, strategically plan the content, type, and form of your activities—naturally keeping all of your activities in line with your brand.

- Stick to your strategy, but keep a critical eye on how things are developing for different channels. They can gain or lose importance very quickly sometimes.

CHAPTER NINE

A PATH FORWARD FOR THE GROWING BUSINESS

FINDING A SUITABLE PARTNER TO BE SUCCESSFUL

■ ■ ■

As the chapters in this book have established, marketing must be a strategic project based on research, experiences, facts and figures, checks and rechecks—and is definitely not something to be taken on using just gut instincts.

As I explained in the early chapters, your strategic marketing efforts should be based on clearly defined parts:

- **Brand:** The unique appearance of your business with

> Marketing must be a strategic project based on research, experiences, facts and figures, checks and rechecks—and is definitely not something to be taken on using just gut instincts.

name, logo, design etc. in order to make your company distinguishable and increase your customers' recognition

- **Buyer Personas:** Representative for the groups to whom you want to direct your marketing

- **Unique Selling Proposition:** What you offer that your competitors do not

I highly recommend that you summarize these insights about your business, customers, and unique offerings in a marketing plan. This will help because writing helps you to sort out your thoughts and think things through. It will help your employees because as soon as the plan is written down, everybody can refer to it and make sure what they're doing is on track with the company's approach to marketing.

Your marketing plan should consist of the following:

- A description of the current situation—the market, the group you want to target with your marketing, and a description of the competition

- An analysis of your company's strengths, weaknesses, opportunities, and threats (SWOT) in comparison with your competitors

- A clear definition of your unique selling proposition (USP)

- A well-thought-out list of SMART goals for your strategic marketing project—specific, measurable, achievable, realistic, and timely goals

- A clear definition of your strategy for reaching these SMART goals

- A marketing budget and a definition of the channels you plan to use to reach your target group

- A system of regular check-ins to ensure that you're staying on the right track

AN EXAMPLE OF A MARKETING PLAN

Let's say you're a hairdresser opening a new shop in a small town where there is already significant competition for hairdressing customers.

The SWOT analysis shows the following:

STRENGTHS

Yours: A strong focus on young middle-aged women who are willing to spend money on hair care; an experienced staff that can offer high quality to this target group.

Your Competitors': Low prices.

WEAKNESSES

Yours: New in the market; has yet to prove quality for the target group; it can be difficult to compete with low prices.

Your Competitors': Low quality goes along with the low prices, so they are vulnerable to competition in that area.

OPPORTUNITIES

Yours: A strict focus on the target group could win clients away from the competition's low-quality work.

Your competitors': Can hire additional experienced staff to better serve your target group.

THREATS

Yours: Due to economic problems, the target group may not be willing to spend more money on hairdressing, so competitors' lower prices could win out.

Your Competitors': Low prices won't necessarily overcome low quality because good hair is important to your target group, and they may be willing to test out a new offering.

USP

Your laser focus on the one target group of young middle-aged women with high budgets who are willing to spend money to look good, and you have the staff with proven expertise who can fulfill these women's desire for better hair care.

SMART GOALS

Specific: Over the next six months, create a pool of fifty faithful customers who are willing to pay a higher price for top-quality hair styling.

Measurable: Monitor the number of clients coming in and how much they spend per person.

Achievable: Based on your current staff and the market situation, this goal can be accomplished.

Realistic and timely: Half a year is a realistic period of time over which to create a solid customer base.

STRATEGY AND ACTIVITIES

- Make sure the shop has a strong presence on important platforms for reaching the target group, with correct and actual data—especially regarding hours of operation.

- Set up a website that is responsive and optimized for search engines, featuring the latest hairstyles and hair care advice for the target group.

- Actively pursuing ratings and reviews—in written form, but also with pictures included—to be published on Google, Facebook, and your website.

- Set up a Facebook page that features weekly information about hair care and hairstyles—and support it with Facebook ads.

- Collect email data and set up a mail program to continually address the target group with news, advice, photos, special offers, etc.

MARKETING BUDGET

When setting up the budget, please include a budget for a website, a mailing provider, an external writer, and a Facebook campaign.

CONTROLLING THROUGH CHECK-INS

Monitoring key performance indicators and conversions should always be on your mind.

Continually review your marketing plan by calculating the ROI for what you're putting into the marketing effort. It may turn out that you've misjudged the market situation or the target group or have made unsound marketing decisions, and these need to be corrected ASAP. Monitoring key performance indicators and conversions should always be on your mind to help you determine whether you're following the right marketing path. (For more information on this, refer to chapter 5.)

THE FOUR Ps

Traditional marketing approaches always include the four Ps, a marketing concept developed back in 1960 by E. Jerome McCarthy that has not lost its relevance to marketing in the digital age. I will list the four Ps here and suggest some chapters in this book where you can learn more about dealing with them:[56]

- **Price:** What do you charge for your products and services? In order to determine this, you need to check out what level of pricing is competitive in your market. Please refer to chapter 3 for more on pricing.

- **Product:** What are you selling? How can you be successful in your market? Please refer to chapter 3 to learn more about dealing with this element of marketing.

- **Promotion:** How do you find your customers? How can your customers find you? Please refer to chapters 4, 5, 7 and 8.

- **Place:** Which distribution channels are most appropriate for your products and services as well as for your company? Please refer to chapter 6 to learn more about selling online.

---

56   For additional reading regarding the Four Ps, please visit "The Four Ps," by Alexandra Twin, on Investopedia, accessed September 2021, https://www.investopedia.com/terms/f/four-ps.asp.

Considering these four Ps is also very helpful when you're setting up your marketing plan and trying to determine how to promote your business.

SOLID GROUND AND CONSTANT RECHECKING

Even after thoroughly thinking about your business, your goals, and how to reach them, you are not spared the need to constantly reflect on the correctness of your assumptions, your orientation, and the marketing plan you are following. It is important that you understand and consider what you're doing in the context of the complete **customer journey**, from getting the potential customer's attention to retaining that customer's loyalty. Having set your marketing plan on solid ground, you also need to consider what the next steps will be to grow your business and then set up goals for one year, three years, and five years.

I highly recommend using the so-called PDCA Cycle or Deming Cycle as your foundation for this process:

The PDCA Cycle

Plan

Do

Check

Act

This management philosophy originated with the US physician Walter Andrew Shewhart and his student William Edwards Deming and is a method meant to be used to increase quality in all parts of a company, from working processes to improving products and services, by continually repeating the cycle of planning, implementing, reviewing, and implementing new ideas and processes.[57]

You also should be continually rechecking your assumptions about marketing your business, and you should also be aware that digital marketing is constantly changing. Some of the ways it's always changing are:

- Search engines such as Google constantly rewrite the rules for ranking companies in their searches in order to improve search results for their users. Google's updates make web developers sweat because sometimes the changes to search engine ranking criteria can completely ruin those developers' efforts to get higher rankings.

- The number and variety of platforms where customers or prospects are searching for your company are constantly increasing, which makes it very hard for you to have your company data listed correctly in all the places it needs to be found.

- The search behavior and media consumption of your target group are rapidly and constantly changing. The portals where you have met them successfully may suddenly be less popular with them, and they may have moved on to a new portal.

---

57 For more information on the PDCA cycle and how to use it, please refer to the PDCA's official website www.pdcahome.com and review their article, "PDCA Cycle (Plan, Do, Check, Act): The Deming Cycle and the Continuous Improvement" at https://pdcahome.com/english/267/pdca-cycle-continuous-improvement/; accessed September 2021.

For a business owner, it may be simply impossible to stay ahead of all the rapid changes in digital marketing. For that reason, I highly recommend that you turn to a professional agency for the knowledge and support you require.

WHEN DO I NEED HELP? UNDERSTANDING MARKETING AS A SERVICE (MAAS)

It is obvious to most companies that they need to hire a professional legal advisor and tax consultant to get the best expert advice about legal requirements and taxes. But it is still not that obvious to many companies that they need to hire outside marketing experts to get professional advice on developing marketing strategies and campaigns or building professional websites that can actually be found and rated highly by search engines.

Especially for small businesses, it can be very helpful to get outside support to supplement internal marketing capacities or to get skills not available in the company. Usually, SMBs do not even have a dedicated marketing person, or, if they do, this person is tasked with the whole bandwidth of marketing-related issues and does not have time to think about new approaches or to acquire the latest skills required to do effective online marketing. (Even larger companies can require outside help when they are entering a new market, launching a new product, or need certain skills not available within their staff.)

THE ADVANTAGES OF MAAS

The advantages of employing an outside marketing team include:

- **Know-how:** Although you know your business inside-out, as an SMB, you probably lack the expertise regarding marketing issues. And even if you have a marketing manager on your team, that manager probably has a limited range of skills and may not be up to dealing with fast-changing marketing issues. Outside support allows you to get the latest marketing insights and techniques—for example, Google's latest (and ever-changing) ranking policies. It takes a lot of time and expertise to always be up to date on things such as the latest developments in marketing on the many platforms available, on **search engine advertising**, and on many other areas of online marketing.

- **New thinking:** It can be very valuable to get input from an outside source because it inspires new thinking about and new approaches to marketing. Because they are not "business-blind," limited by preconceptions about your business and industry, outside experts can come up with interesting new ideas to help you grow your business.

- **Flexibility:** Instead of going through all the effort of developing full-blown internal marketing skills within your company, it might be more efficient to hire outside experts when you really need them.

- **Productivity and time management:** When you hire a legal or tax advisor, it is obvious you are doing this to save time, to get the best expert advice, and to allow you to take care of your core business. The same is true for hiring external marketing expertise. Additionally, projects assigned to outside providers get those providers' complete focus and are therefore conducted in a more efficient and timely manner than you can do it internally. Even if you are willing to hire a marketing manager, consider the time and effort required to first search for and find the right person, to get him or her on board and prepared to finally start working on your marketing projects. Outside marketing teams are ready to go at a moment's notice.

* **Cost:** It may seem that hiring outside help would be a financial burden; however, you should consider the income to be gained from allowing yourself to focus on improving your business, finding more and better ways to serve your customers. Even if you have a marketing manager on your team, hiring outside help for special projects can be worthwhile and cost effective because your manager can focus on the marketing work that is not easily transferred to outside experts. Additionally, the costs for outside support can be calculated in advance so that a cost overview is always available and can be taken into account in your finances.

WHAT TO KEEP IN MIND WHEN YOU CHOOSE A MAAS SOLUTION

Before choosing a MaaS provider, you need to determine what you or your staff can easily do yourself and where you need external help; the exact areas and kinds of skills where you need that help; what you expect from your MaaS provider in a written contract, including an NDA (nondisclosure agreement); and whether you want several providers of services or a one-stop shop.

Especially for SMBs, a one-stop shop is highly recommended; it is more cost effective and less time consuming because you only have to explain your business once instead of again and again for each provider. It is also easier to handle one business partner instead of several. A one-stop shop can give advice about which marketing efforts could be effective for you and which you are better off avoiding. And with a one-stop shop, the marketing activities tie into one another because one provider is dealing with all of them. A one-stop shop is also valuable for bigger enterprises when they are launching highly sophisticated individual marketing projects—some of which are described in previous chapters of this book.

FCR MEDIA: THE ADVANTAGES OF A ONE-STOP SHOP

FCR Media in Belgium, the company I have been working for since 2016, is an excellent example of a one-stop digital marketing agency. With more than twenty-five thousand customers in seventeen hundred business segments, the digital consultants at FCR Media know the challenges businesses—and especially SMBs—are facing in digital marketing today.

It is part of company policy that each customer can rely on a designated account manager who takes care of all areas of concern the customer has. The range of digital services is wide, including everything from designing websites and web shops to search engine and social media campaigns to using CRM tools. As a partner of Google, Bing, and Facebook, FCR Media can offer the latest products and insights in digital marketing to their customers. Thanks to goudengids.be, FCR can even provide its own portal for local searches as an efficient advertising platform for SMBs.

Providing all necessary products and services, FCR Media is the kind of one-stop shop that an SMB needs to grow its business through digital marketing. The feedback from customers is the best proof of the level of FCR's daily support for SMBs. Many small manufacturers have grown their businesses with FCR's assistance. The following story shows how successful the relationship between an SMB and a one-stop shop can be.

When founding his business, a young plumber turned to the agency I worked for in those days. Because he didn't have his own office or even a desk, he had to sign the first contract with his media consultant on the hood of his car. Ten years later, he had shops in each province of the country and was serving a large clientele with a lot of employees. When he celebrated his anniversary, he only invited a few people who had helped him to become so successful. And among those select guests was the media consultant from my agency who had advised the plumber on the marketing decisions that helped him grow his business to such a great extent. The plumber/CEO recognized that he would not have achieved that level of success without the solid marketing advice that our company provided him. We were an integral factor in his success.

TERMS TO KNOW

■   ■   ■

A/B testing

This is a common procedure to achieve optimal results of communication: One or more elements of a subject (mailing, blog, website, letter etc.) are deliberately changed to see how the outcome can be improved.

Backlinks

Backlinks are links from different websites to your own website. The number of backlinks can influence the ranking of your website in search engines, provided these are high-quality links.

Blacklist

This term is used in email marketing. It is a list of mailing addresses for which sending mails is forbidden.

Bounce rates

The bounce rate indicates how many website visitors visit one page and then leave the site immediately without surfing to other subpages (see "Subpage" entry).

Buyer/customer personas

Personas are a generalized representation of your average customer. It is a picture of a typical customer based on information collected while doing business with all of your customers and prospects. The customer personas enable you to target your broadest marketing and customer acquisition efforts.

Call to action (CTA)

A call to action (CTA) is a clear and obvious request for a user to take a certain action. It is highly used in all forms of digital communication (mailings, websites, blogs etc.) and usually consists of a prominently placed button indicating what to do next, such as opening a landing page, making a phone call, filling out a form, etc.

Content management system (CMS)

A CMS is a software that enables the creation and editing of content on a website. Most of them allow the upload of pictures and videos in addition to placing and editing text.

Content marketing

Content marketing is a very common marketing technique: its aim is to provide highly valuable content to customers or prospects to convince them of the expertise and competence of a certain company. For example, blogs are common tools of content marketing.

Common payment models of online advertising

Cost-per-Impression: Cost for a visual contact or the page retrieval of an entire HTML document with a browser—page impressions are usually not assigned to a specific user.

Cost-per-Mille: Cost per thousand impressions.

Cost-per-View: Cost for every instance an ad or video is seen—the pricing is used in online marketing, social media marketing, and video marketing; in video marketing, metrics usually only count if the viewer engages with the video and clicks on the play or skip button.

Cost-per-Click: Cost for a click on an ad; this is very common and used on many portals.

Cost-per-Lead: Cost for a special predefined action, such as a newsletter registration or a download.

Cost-per-Order or **Cost-per-Sale:** Cost-per-order or purchase.

Cookie

A cookie is a small piece of data/pixel that is used to identify your PC, laptop, etc., as you use a website. This way, information about your behavior—such as which topics are looked at, which links are used, etc.—on the site is collected.

Customer journey

Customer journey describes the different phases a customer goes through from their first encounter with a brand until purchasing a product or service.

Home page

This is the initial page of a website.

HTTPS (Hypertext transfer protocol secure)

Internet communication protocol that makes sure the data transfer (passwords, text messages, credit card information, etc.) between your computer and the server(s) you're sending this data to is safe.

Keywords

Keywords are essential in search engine optimization (see "search engine optimization [SEO]" entry) and online marketing, especially search engine advertising (SEA). Entered in the search field of a search engine, the keyword is matched by search algorithms. A list of results for this keyword is shown on the search results page (SERP). There are short- and long-tail keywords. **Short-tail keywords** are rather short phrases like "lawn mower buying." Because of their less precise significance, they generate a high volume of search results. In comparison, **long-tail keywords** are longer phrases with more details like "electric rear engine riding lawn mower," which generate more distinctive results.

Link

A link or hyperlink is a cross-reference between two websites or to a certain position of a document.

Remarketing/retargeting

Visitors to websites are tracked using cookies in order to show them advertising that might be especially interesting to them.

ROPO (research online, purchase offline)

The term addresses the habit of consumers to get online information about the products and services they intend to buy but to actually purchase the goods in a real store.

Search engine advertising (SEA)

SEA is an advertising method displaying ads in search engine results whenever someone searches for certain services or products. On Google, these ads appear on the top or on the far-right side of a search-result page.

Search engine marketing (SEM)

SEM describes all activities in search engines to raise the interest of a certain target group for a special web offering. Search engine advertising (SEA) and search engine optimization (SEO) are the two methods of SEM to achieve this goal.

Search engine optimization (SEO)

SEO strategies and techniques make sure that your website is listed in a top position on the search results page of a search engine.

Secure socket layer (SSL)

SSL is used to ensure data (passwords, text messages, credit card information etc.) transferred across the internet from computer to computer is safe.

Subpage

Subpages are a way to structure your website: They are subordinate to your home page and may consist of "Products and Services," "About Us," "News," etc.

Website

A website is the center of your online presence. It is a collection of several pages (subpages) which can be accessed with a domain name.

ABOUT THE AUTHOR

■　　■　　■

Jon Martinsen was born in Oslo, Norway, in 1964 and studied at Oslo Business School, focusing on finance and marketing. Since 1987, he has worked in the local search industry with roles in IT, finance, operations, business development, sales, marketing, and general/executive management. Because of this varied background, he has a 360-degree view of a business and knows what is needed to be successful.

Today, Jon Martinsen is the CEO of FCR Media Group, which has offices in Estonia, the Czech Republic, Romania, Croatia, Belgium, and the Netherlands. He has lived in Oslo, Stockholm, Amsterdam, Tallinn, and Vienna and has also worked across Finland, Latvia, Lithuania, Slovakia, Hungary, Ireland, the Netherlands, and Uruguay. This background in combination with his current activities has given him experience with many cultures, so he understands the universal problems that many businesses face.

In particular, he has witnessed the rapid change caused by digital marketing meaning major challenges especially for SMBs. They now have to deal with search engines, social media, web shops, etc., which can be very confusing and time consuming for a business owner who basically has to run their business. To make their lives a little easier, Jon Martinsen decided to write this book and explain the marketing basics an SMB should know.

Jon Martinsen is married, has two sons, and currently lives in Austria. Like many successful managers, he loves spending his leisure time doing different types of sports, first and foremost skiing, and is pursuing athletic goals as ambitiously as business goals.

CPSIA information can be obtained
at www.ICGtesting.com
Printed in the USA
BVHW091749040522
636153BV00010B/31

9 781642 253597